GROWING STRONG IN GOD'S FAMILY

THE 2:7 SERIES

NAVPRESS ⬧®

A MINISTRY OF THE NAVIGATORS

P.O. BOX 35001, COLORADO SPRINGS, COLORADO 80935

The Navigators is an international Christian organization. Jesus Christ gave His followers the Great Commission to go and make disciples (Matthew 28:19). The aim of The Navigators is to help fulfill that commission by multiplying laborers for Christ in every nation.

NavPress is the publishing ministry of The Navigators. NavPress publications are tools to help Christians grow. Although publications alone cannot make disciples or change lives, they can help believers learn biblical discipleship, and apply what they learn to their lives and ministries.

ISBN 08910-91653

Ninth printing, 1992

Unless otherwise identified, Scripture quotations are from the *Holy Bible: New International Version* (NIV). Copyright © 1973, 1978, 1984, International Bible Society. Used by permission of Zondervan Bible Publishers. Other versions quoted are the *Amplified New Testament* (AMP), © The Lockman Foundation 1954, 1958; *The Modern Language Bible: The Berkeley Version in Modern English* (BERK), © 1945, 1959, 1969, by Zondervan Publishing House; the *King James Version* (KJV); *The Living Bible* (LB), © 1971 by Tyndale House Publishers, Wheaton, Illinois, and used by permission; the *New American Standard Bible* (NASB), © The Lockman Foundation 1960, 1962, 1963, 1968, 1971, 1972, 1973, 1975, 1977; *The New Testament in Modern English, Revised Edition* by J. B. Phillips (PH), © 1958, 1960, 1972, by J. B. Phillips; and the *Revised Standard Version of the Bible* (RSV), copyrighted 1946, 1952, © 1971, 1973.

Printed in the United States of America

Important

1. LEADER'S GUIDE

It is important for one person to act as the leader during each group meeting. This may be the same person each time or the responsibility may be shared by two or three group members.

There is a leader's guide for *Growing Strong in God's Family* in the back of this book. It is important for the group leader to use this material each week as a part of his or her careful preparation.

2. LEADER TRAINING CLINICS

Excellent leader training clinics are available once or twice a year in many areas of the United States, Canada, and several other countries. Those who have invested a few hours in a leader training clinic will be able to maximize the effectiveness of *Growing Strong in God's Family*.

Attendance at a leadership training clinic is not required in order to use *Growing Strong in God's Family*. However, to continue in the *2:7 Series* courses, leaders must attend a training clinic.

Information about training clinics may be obtained from Church Discipleship Ministries, The Navigators, P.O. Box 6000, Colorado Springs, CO 80934. The telephone number is (719) 598-1212. Or contact The Navigators of Canada, Unit 12—270 Esna Park Drive, Markham, ON, L3R 1H3, CANADA. The telephone number is (416) 475-0300.

ACKNOWLEDGMENT: We are grateful for the dedicated efforts of Ron Oertli who originated the concept of *Growing Strong in God's Family* and *The 2:7 Series* and is their principal author.

Contents

FOLLOWING PAGE 115 YOU WILL FIND THESE WORKSHEETS:
BIBLE READING HIGHLIGHTS RECORDS, MY PERSONAL READING RECORD
AND SCRIPTURE MEMORY CARDS.

Completion Record

Ask others in your study group to check you on your completion of the requirements in this course and have them initial and date each section.

SCRIPTURE MEMORY	Initial	Date
Beginning with Christ memory verses:		
"Assurance of Salvation"—1 John 5:11-12		
"Assurance of Answered Prayer"—John 16:24		
"Assurance of Victory"—1 Corinthians 10:13		
"Assurance of Forgiveness"—1 John 1:9		
"Assurance of Guidance"—Proverbs 3:5-6		
Quoted all *Beginning with Christ Verses*		
Reviewed *Beginning with Christ* for 7 consecutive days		
Completed the *Beginning with Christ* Bible Study		

QUIET TIME		
Completed *Bible Reading Highlights Record* for 7 consecutive days		

BIBLE STUDY—*The Wheel Illustration*		
Session 2—*Beginning with Christ* Bible Study		
Session 3—"Christ the Center"		
Session 4—"Obedience"		
Session 6—"The Word"		
Session 8—"Prayer"		
Session 9—"Fellowship"		
Session 10—"Witness"		

BOOKLET STUDIED		
Tyranny of the Urgent		
Completed pages 23-24		

MISCELLANEOUS		
Completed the Evaluation of the Wheel page 69		
Completed Why Memorize Scripture page 70		
Completed the Evangelism Prayer List page 47		

LEADER'S CHECK		
Five entries on the *Bible Reading Highlights Record*		
Graduated from *Growing Strong in God's Family*		

Session 1

How Growing Strong in God's Family *Came About*

A few years ago The Navigators introduced a dynamic lay training concept called *The 2:7 Series* (the name comes from the Scripture reference Colossians 2:7). It was the product of much prayer, effort and repeated fieldtesting. It consisted of a series of six, 12-week courses. Thousands of church laypeople in the United States, Canada, and several other countries received this training.

Extensive use of *The 2:7 Series* revealed the need for something like *Growing Strong in God's Family*—a course with strong content and practicality that could be taken without an obligation to do the whole *2:7 Series*.

Growing Strong in God's Family gives you the opportunity to learn and practice some of the most helpful concepts taught in the original *2:7 Series*. It will spiritually refresh you and strengthen your Christian foundation.

The new, revised *2:7 Series* consists of five 11-week courses. Courses 1 and 2 emphasize *The Growing Disciple*. Courses 3-5 focus on *The Ministering Disciple*. It is important for a person to complete *Growing Strong in God's Family* before beginning Course 1 in *The 2:7 Series*.

Growing Strong in God's Family was written to impact a broad spectrum of local church men and women. It is not too difficult for a person who has been a Christian for only a few months. Yet, the content and practicality are challenging enough for the person who has been a Christian for several years. Enjoy!

General Comments

1. There should be eight to ten students in most class groups to enable them to have the best personal attention. This will also create a more informal atmosphere.
2. No one should join the group after Session 2.
3. You must complete certain requirements to graduate from this course. While not difficult, graduation will require purposeful effort. Plan to graduate.
4. Keep in mind that anything truly worthwhile will be costly in some way.
5. Most class sessions will require about one hour of preparation time.
6. If you complete your assigned work on time, you will find the training more enjoyable. You will also derive more permanent benefit from the course.
7. You will not want to miss more than two sessions. It is difficult to catch up once you get behind.
8. This is not a lecture course. You will have an opportunity to participate in every session.

How to Mark Your Bible as You Read

You should obtain an inexpensive Bible with heavier paper for your reading and marking. Choose a contemporary translation or paraphrase.

You can use a ballpoint or a fine felt-tip pen to mark your Bible with the following symbols:

1. Brackets— [ ]
2. Short diagonal lead-in— \
3. Parallel diagonal lines in the margin— ⁄⁄
4. Circles— ◯
5. Vertical lines in the margin— |
6. Underlining— _____

As another option, you may use a "highlighter" to mark through the words you want to draw attention to instead of underlining them.

You may choose to use all of these markings as you read, you may choose to use only one or two of your favorite ones, or you may choose to make up some of your own.

In the following four passages of Scripture marking is illustrated.

ISAIAH 11:1-7

A shoot will come up from the stump of Jesse; from his roots a Branch will bear fruit. ²The Spirit of the Lord will rest on him—[the Spirit of wisdom and of understanding, the Spirit of counsel and of power, the Spirit of knowledge and of the fear of the Lord]— ³and he will delight in the fear of the Lord. He will not judge by what he sees with his eyes, or decide by what he hears with his ears; ⁴but with righteousness he will judge the needy, with justice he will give decisions for the poor of the earth. He will strike the earth with the rod of his mouth; with the breath of his lips he will slay the wicked. Righteousness will be his belt and faithfulness the sash around his waist. ⁶The wolf will live with the lamb, the leopard will lie down with the goat, the calf and the lion and the yearling together; and a little child will lead them. ⁷The cow will feed with the bear, their young will lie down together, and the lion will eat straw like the ox.

LUKE 5:15-17

¹⁵Yet the news about him spread all the more, so that crowds of people came to hear him and to be healed of their sicknesses. ¹⁶But Jesus often

withdrew to lonely places and prayed.

17One day as he was teaching, Pharisees and teachers of the law, who had come from every village of Galilee and from Judea and Jerusalem, were sitting there. And the power of the Lord was present for him to heal the sick.

1 KINGS 12:3-9 (BERK)

3When Jeroboam and the whole assembly of Israel arrived, they addressed Rehoboam, saying, 4"Your father made our yoke unbearable. Now lighten the unbearable service of your father and the heavy yoke he laid upon us, and we will serve you." 5He responded, "Give me three more days; then return to me."

When the people left, 6 Rehoboam conferred with the elders who had stood by Solomon when he was still alive, saying, "How would you advise me to reply to the people?" 7They advised him, "If you will be a servant to this people now and serve them and reply to them with kind words, they will always be your servants." 8But he rejected the advice which the elders gave him. Then he conferred with the young men who grew up with him and who stood by him. 9"What do you advise us to say to this people who petitioned me, 'Make lighter the yoke your father laid upon us'?"

1 THESSALONIANS 1:1-7 (AMP)

Paul, Silvanus (Silas) and Timothy to the assembly (church) of the Thessalonians in God the Father and the Lord Jesus Christ, the Messiah: Grace (spiritual blessing and define favor) to you and heart peace.

2We are ever giving thanks to God for all of you, continually mentioning [you when engaged] in our prayers, 3recalling unceasingly before our God and Father your work energized by faith and service motivated by love, and unwavering hope in (the return of) our Lord Jesus Christ, the Messiah. 4[O] brethren beloved by God, we recognize and know that He has selected (chosen) you; 5for our [preaching of the] glad tidings (the Gospel) came to you not only in word, but also in (its own inherent) power and in the Holy Spirit, and with great conviction *and* absolute certainty (on our part). You know what kind of men we proved [ourselves] to be among you for your good. 6And you [set yourselves to] become imitators of us and [through us] of the Lord Himself, for you welcomed our message in [spite of the] much persecution, with joy [inspired] of the Holy Spirit; 7so that you [thus] became a pattern to all the believers—those who adhere to, trust in and rely on Christ Jesus—in Macedonia and Achaia [most of Greece].

Where to Read in Your Bible

1. If reading the Bible is fairly new to you, you should start with books in the New Testament. (Some find the Gospel of Matthew to be difficult reading.)
2. Finish reading all of one book before starting another.
3. Perhaps the two most difficult books in the Bible are Leviticus and Revelation. Put off reading these two books until after *Growing Strong in God's Family.*
4. Instead of reading the Gospels consecutively, intersperse them with other books for variety.
5. When you are ready to begin reading in the Old Testament, you might pick one of the following books: Joshua, 1 Samuel, 2 Samuel, 1 Kings, 2 Kings, Genesis, Daniel.
6. Some Old Testament books have difficult passages, so just skim through those sections.

Reading and Marking Exercise

For your reading and marking exercise, you will now work on Romans 12. As you do this exercise, you will want to:

1. Pray that God will speak to you from His Word.

2. Think through the passage.

3. Mark the thoughts that impress you most.

After you have read this passage, you will have an opportunity to share one or two things that you marked.

ROMANS 12

Therefore, I urge you, brothers, in view of God's mercy, to offer your bodies as living sacrifices, holy and pleasing to God—which is your spiritual worship. [2]Do not conform any longer to the pattern of this world, but be transformed by the renewing of your mind. Then you will be able to test and approve what God's will is—his good, pleasing and perfect will.

[3]For by the grace given me I say to every one of you: Do not think of yourself more highly than you ought, but rather think of yourself with sober judgment, in accordance with the measure of faith God has given you. [4]Just as each of us has one body with many members, and these members do not all have the same function, [5]so in Christ we who are many form one body, and each member belongs to all the others. [6]We have different gifts, according to the grace given us. If a man's gift is prophesying, let him use it in proportion to his faith. [7]If it is serving, let him serve; if it is teaching, let him teach, [8]if it is encouraging, let him encourage; if it is contributing to the needs of others, let him give generously; if it is leadership, let him govern diligently; if it is showing mercy, let him do it cheerfully.

[9]Love must be sincere. Hate what is evil; cling to what is good. [10]Be devoted to one another in brotherly love. Honor one another above yourselves. [11]Never be lacking in zeal, but keep your spiritual fervor, serving the Lord. [12]Be joyful in hope, patient in affliction, faithful in prayer. [13]Share with God's people who are in need. Practice hospitality.

[14]Bless those who persecute you; bless and do not curse. [15]Rejoice with those who rejoice; mourn with those who mourn. [16]Live in harmony with one another. Do not be proud, but be willing to associate with people of low position. Do not be conceited.

[17]Do not repay anyone evil for evil. Be careful to do what is right in the eyes of everybody. [18]If it is possible, as far as it depends on you, live at peace with everyone. [19]Do not take revenge, my friends, but leave room for God's wrath, for it is written: "It is mine to avenge; I will repay," says the Lord. [20]On the contrary:

"If your enemy is hungry, feed him; if he is thirsty, give him something to drink.

In doing this, you will heap burning coals on his head." [21]Do not be overcome by evil, but overcome evil with good.

Beginning with Christ *Explanation*

The Bible says, "That if you confess with your mouth, 'Jesus is Lord,' and believe in your heart that God raised him from the dead, you will be saved. For it is with your heart that you believe and are justified, and it is with your mouth that you confess and are saved" (Romans 10:9-10). Coupled with this wonderful truth is the statement in His Word that "as many as received Him, to them gave He power to become the sons of God" (John 1:12).

If you have to the best of your knowledge received Jesus Christ—trusted Him as your own Savior, according to the Scriptures quoted above you have become a child of God in whom Jesus Christ dwells.

Altogether too many people make the mistake of measuring the certainty of their salvation by their feelings. Don't make this tragic mistake. Believe God. Take Him at His word: "These things have I written unto you that believe on the name of the Son of God; that ye may know that ye have eternal life" (1 John 5:13).

It is impossible in these few pages to go into all the wonderful results of the transaction that took place when you received Christ. A child may be born into a wealthy home and become the possessor of good parents, brothers and sisters, houses and lands, but at the time of his birth it is not necessary that he be informed of all these wonderful things. There are more important matters to take care of first. He must be protected, for he has been born into a world of many enemies. In the hospital room he is handled with sterilized gloves and kept from outsiders that he might not fall victim to the myriad germs waiting to attack. It is the awareness of such enemies which enables the doctors and nurses to take measures to protect the precious new life.

You have become a child of God; you have been born into His family as a spiritual babe. This is a strategic moment in your life. The following basic truths will strengthen you for the battle ahead and keep you safe from the onslaughts of Satan.

In 1 Peter 2:2 you will read, "As newborn babes, desire the sincere milk of the Word, that ye may grow thereby." In Acts 20:32 you will read, "And now, brethren, I commend you to God, and to the Word of His grace which is able to build you up." The Bible will now serve as your spiritual food and will build you up in the faith. In this course, you will be taught how to read your Bible. It is most important that you have time set aside, preferably in the morning, to read the Word of God and pray.

Now let's be more specific with regard to your intake of the Word of God. In Psalm 119 it says, "Wherewithal shall a young man cleanse his way? by taking heed thereto according to Thy Word" (verse 9), and then the psalmist speaks to the Lord saying, "Thy Word have I hid in mine heart, that I might not sin against Thee" (verse 11). So hide His Word in your heart; memorize it. In this course we have included five key passages with which you may begin.

Let us consider for a moment this new enemy which you face. Before you trusted Christ, Satan may not have bothered you particularly, but now he has seen you make the step which angers him more than any one thing in all the world. You have left his crowd and joined the ranks of those who believe and trust in the Son of God. You are no longer in Satan's domain; you now belong to the One who has bought and paid for you with a price, the price of His own blood shed on the cross. You may be sure that Satan will attempt to trouble you. His attacks assume many forms. These verses will help you deal with some of the most common ones and give you help on how to resist him successfully.

You can overcome him only as you use the weapons which God has provided. Paul said, "And take . . . the sword of the Spirit, which is the Word of God" (Ephesians 6:17). The Bible then is the primary weapon against these attacks.

Consider that Jesus Christ was tempted by Satan in three specific ways, and He defeated him each time with Scripture, saying, "It is written . . ." (See Matthew 4). If Christ deemed it necessary to meet Satan this way, how much more do you need this mighty weapon, the Word of God. How much more you need to be prepared to say to Satan, "It is written . . ." or "Thus said the Lord . . ."

1. ASSURANCE OF SALVATION

The memory verses of Scripture in this course have been chosen to equip you for your first few encounters with the enemy and to encourage you to trust God daily. Satan's first approach is often to cast doubt upon the work which God has done in your heart. You may find yourself thinking; "How can I be saved and my sins forgiven just by believing and receiving Christ? Surely that is not enough!"

Your only hope to withstand such an attack is to resort to God's Word. What does God say about the matter? That is the important thing. And so the first memory passage, 1 John 5:11-12 entitled Assurance of Salvation, says: "And this is the record, that God hath given to us eternal life, and this life is in His Son. He that hath the Son hath life; and he that hath not the Son of God hath not life."

When this passage has been written on the table of your heart you will be able to use it every time a doubt arises. On the basis of God's written Word, you will have overcome one of the first tests. This attack may recur, but now you have the Word of God in your heart with which to meet it.

2. ASSURANCE OF ANSWERED PRAYER

Another attack of Satan may be to cause you to doubt the effectiveness of prayer. You may catch yourself thinking, "How can God be really personally interested in me? He seems far away and is probably concerned about more important things. Does he hear me when I pray—much less answer my prayers?"

Now that Jesus Christ is your Savior and Lord you have the unique privilege of speaking directly with your heavenly Father through Him. He wants you to come confidently into His presence (Hebrews 4:16) and to talk to Him about everything (Philippians 4:6). He is intensely interested in you and your needs. In the second passage, John 16:24, Jesus gives us His Assurance of Answered Prayer: "Hitherto have ye asked nothing in My Name; ask, and ye shall receive, that your joy may be full."

Jesus did not say His disciples had never asked before. You yourself have probably asked may times, especially when in trouble. But now you can ask in Jesus' name, because you belong to Him. To ask in His Name means to ask in His authority and on His merit. Just as the Father answered Jesus' every prayer, so will He answer you when you ask in Jesus' Name. He delights to answer your call and meet your needs. Memorize this wonderful promise. Apply its truth and experience the joy of answered prayer.

3. ASSURANCE OF VICTORY

Still another attack may be along this line. "I have life, all right, but I am a weakling; I have always been a weakling."

You will remember some sin which has gripped you throughout the past years of your life. You will think, "I am weak; I will not be able to stand against this particular temptation. Perhaps I have been able to stand against others, but not this one."

How will you answer this doubt? Will you rely on what this person or that one says, or will you resort to the invincible Word? The third passage, 1 Corinthians 10:13, is chosen especially to meet this attack of Satan: "There hath no temptation taken you but such as is common to man, but God is faithful, who will not suffer you to be tempted

above that ye are able; but will with the temptation also make a way to escape, that ye may be able to bear it."

This gives Assurance of Victory. God promises victory over temptation. It belongs to you as a child of His. Believe what God has said and you will see that things impossible with men are possible with God. It will thrill you to see that chains of lifetime habits can be broken by His mighty power. Memorize this verse; write it on the table of your heart, then trust the Holy Spirit to help you live victoriously over sin.

4. ASSURANCE OF FORGIVENESS

This brings us to the next attack of Satan. Although victory over temptation is rightfully yours, you may fail. When you sin, you may think, "Now I've done it. I'm supposed to be a Christian but Christians don't do those things, do they?"

Nevertheless, God makes provision in His Word for the failures of His children, and so the fourth passage speaks of the Assurance of Forgiveness, 1 John 1:9: "If we confess our sins, He is faithful and just to forgive us our sins, and to cleanse us from all unrighteousness."

To confess a sin means to uncover it by calling it exactly what God calls it. Implicit in honest confession is the willingness to forsake the sin (Proverbs 28:13). God promises not only to forgive us, but also to cleanse us. What a gracious provision!

5. ASSURANCE OF GUIDANCE

The four preceding assurances have been given to help you meet the principal attacks of Satan. However, the fifth passage for you to memorize is for a different purpose.

You may have questions about the future, wondering how this new life of yours is all going to work out. "What about God's will for my life? Will He really lead me?" Hence, this verse comes to give you Assurance of Guidance, Proverbs 3:5-6.

"Trust in the Lord with all thine heart; and lean not unto thine own understanding. In all thy ways acknowledge Him, and He shall direct thy paths."

God promises to lead you and direct your path when you rely on Him completely. Memorize and apply this Scripture as a reminder to trust God for His guidance in your life.

    After you have memorized these verses and learned to apply them, you will be aware of the strength and blessing that comes from hiding God's Word in your heart.

How to Memorize a Verse Effectively

GUIDELINES FOR MEMORIZING A VERSE OF SCRIPTURE

1. Before you start to memorize the verse, read it aloud several times.
2. Learn the topic, reference, and the first phrase as a unit.
3. After you have reviewed the topic, reference, and first phrase a few times, add the second phrase. Gradually add phrases until you know the whole verse.
4. Work on the verses audibly whenever possible.
5. As you memorize and review the verse, think about how it applies to your own life.
6. Always review the verse in this sequence:
   - a. TOPIC: "Assurance of Salvation"
   - b. REFERENCE: "First John five, eleven and twelve"
   - c. VERSE(S):   "And this is the testimony: God has given us eternal life, and this life is in his Son. He who has the Son has life; he who does not have the Son of God does not have life."
   - d. REFERENCE: "First John five, eleven and twelve"
7. a. The most critical element in scripture memory is REVIEW, REVIEW, REVIEW. The most important time to review a verse repeatedly is right after you can quote the whole verse (topic, reference, verse, reference) without making a mistake. Review the verse a minimum of once daily after that, preferably several times a day. The more you review the greater your retention.

   b. The most important concept is the principle of OVERLEARNING. A verse should not be considered memorized simply at the point when we can quote it accurately. Only when we have reviewed it frequently enough for it to become *ingrained* in our memory should we consider a verse memorized.

ASSIGNMENT FOR SESSION 2:

1. Scripture Memory: Carefully read the *Beginning with Christ* Explanation (pages 10-13). Memorize the passage on "Assurance of Salvation," 1 John 5:11-12.
2. Bible Reading: Obtain a contemporary translation or paraphrase of the Bible. Read and mark in it each day.
3. Bible Study: Complete the "*Beginning with Christ* Bible Study" (pages 15-17).

Session 2

OUTLINE OF THIS SESSION:
1. Get further acquainted with one another.
2. Review Session 1.
3. Share with the rest of the class what you have read and marked in your Bible this week.
4. Break into small groups to review your memory verses—1 John 5:11-12.
5. Review memory methods:
   a. Practice aloud.
   b. Spot and correct repeated errors.
   c. Review is the key. Do it daily!
6. Read "Introduction To Bible Study" (page 14-15) and look over the first study, "Christ The Center" (pages 24-28).
7. Discuss the "*Beginning with Christ* Bible Study" (pages 15-17).
8. Read the Assignment for Session 3 (page 18).
9. Close the session in prayer.

Introduction to Bible Study

One-third of the world's people go to bed hungry. It's also tragic to be one of the many who go through life spiritually undernourished. The words Jesus spoke centuries ago are still true, "Man does not live on bread alone, but on every word that comes from the mouth of God" (Matthew 4:4).

Because they recognize this hunger of heart that only God's Word can satisfy, more and more people are turning to serious study of the Bible. Both those new to the Christian faith and those who have known Christ for many years need this divinely appointed food for spiritual health and growth.

The Bible studies used here in *Growing Strong in God's Family* have been carefully worked out to help you:
- establish a program of personal study of God's Word.
- examine the great truths of the Bible.
- learn and practice the essentials of discipleship.

All you need to begin is a Bible. The questions will direct you to a passage of Scripture. After considering the Scripture, write the answer in your own words. Scripture references will give the book, chapter, and verse(s). For example, Acts 20:32 refers to the Book of Acts, chapter 20, verse 32.

14

Be sure to pray before you begin your study. Ask the Lord for understanding as you study. "Open my eyes that I may see wonderful things in your law." Psalm 119:18

For your personal Bible study, you need:

A TIME: Just as church attendance is planned for a regular time each week, you should plan a time for your Bible study. Some like to study a little every day; others set aside an evening each week. Decide on a time that is best for you, then stick to it faithfully.

A PLACE: Choose a place free from distractions. If possible, study in the same place each time.

METHOD: As you consider each verse of Scripture, think about it carefully, then write out your answer. It's also helpful to read the context (the surrounding verses) of each passage listed. Write the answers in your own words whenever possible.

MATERIAL: Beside your study book, you will need a complete Bible—Old and New Testaments.
Use a translation, not a paraphrase.

Beginning with Christ *Bible Study*

Complete the following questions based on your reading *Beginning with Christ* Explanation.

1. The five topics and references of the verses you will be memorizing during *Growing Strong in God's Family* are:

	TOPIC	REFERENCE
Assurance of	_____	_____
Assurance of	_____	_____
Assurance of	_____	_____
Assurance of	_____	_____
Assurance of	_____	_____

2. What is one truth taught about salvation in both Romans 10:9-10 and John 1:12? (page 10)

_____

3. Complete the following sentence (page 10): "Altogether too many people make the mistake of measuring the certainty of their salvation _____ ."

4. Complete the following sentence (1 Peter 2:2; Acts 20:32; page 11): "His Word will now serve as your _____ and will _____ in the faith."

5. The psalmist said, "I have hidden your word in my heart" (Psalm 119:11). What do you think that means? (page 11)

_____

_____

6. What effective weapon has God provided for use against Satan's attacks? (Ephesians 6:17, page 11)

_____

7. What did Jesus say to Satan in a time of temptation? (page 11)

_____

_____

The five verses you will memorize and study in *Growing Strong in God's Family* will help equip you for your encounters with our enemy, Satan. Complete the following questions.

ASSURANCE OF SALVATION

8. How would you define eternal life? John 17:3

_____

_____

9. Exploring 1 John 5:11-12 (page 11)

   a. Who gives eternal life? _____

   b. Where is eternal life found? _____

   c. Who has eternal life? _____

   d. Who does not have eternal life? _____

ASSURANCE OF ANSWERED PRAYER

10. Write a definition of prayer. _____

_____

11. Exploring John 16:24 (page 12)

   a. What did Jesus identify as a major need in the disciples' lives?

   _____

   b. In whose name should we pray and why? _____

   _____

   c. What results from prayer? _____

   _____

ASSURANCE OF VICTORY

12. How would you define temptation? _____

_____

_____

_____

_____

13. Exploring 1 Corinthians 10:13 (page 12)

    a. What is true about every temptation you face? _____

_____

    b. Who can give you victory when you are tempted? _____

_____

    c. What does God do for you? _____

_____

ASSURANCE OF FORGIVENESS

14. Why is forgiveness important? _____

_____

15. Exploring 1 John 1:9 (page 12)

    a. What does God want you to do if you sin? _____

_____

    b. What does it mean to confess? _____

_____

    c. In His act of forgiving us, how is God described? _____

_____

    d. What else does God do when you confess a sin? _____

_____

ASSURANCE OF GUIDANCE

16. What are some ways you have seen God guide people?

_____

_____

_____

17. Exploring Proverbs 3:5-6 (page 12)

    a. What three things are you told to do?

_____

_____

_____

    b. When these conditions are met, what are you promised?

_____

_____

ASSIGNMENT FOR SESSION 3:

1. Scripture Memory: Memorize the verse on "Assurance of Answered Prayer," John 16:24.
2. Bible Reading: Continue reading and marking your Bible.
3. Bible Study: Complete the Bible study, "Christ The Center" (pages 24-28).
4. Other: Carefully read and mark the article *Tyranny of the Urgent* by Charles E. Hummell on pages 20-23. Complete numbers 1, 2, 3, and 5 on " A Discussion of *Tyranny of the Urgent"* on pages 23-24.

Session 3

OUTLINE OF THIS SESSION:

1. Study "How to Review Memory Verses Together" (pages 19-20).
2. Break into groups of two or three and review your memory verses:
   a. "Assurance of Salvation"—1 John 5:11-12
   b. "Assurance of Answered Prayer"—John 16:24
3. Share with the rest of the class what you have read and marked in your Bible this week.
4. Discuss the article *Tyranny of the Urgent* (pages 20-24).
5. Discuss the Bible study, "Christ The Center" (pages 24-28).
6. Go over "How to Use *My Personal Reading Record*" (pages 28-29). Locate *My Personal Reading Record* following page 115.
7. Read the "Assignment for Session 4" (page 29).
8. Close the session in prayer.

How to Review Memory Verses Together

1. Review the memory verses you know best first. This helps to build confidence.
2. Maintain an attitude of helpfulness, encouragement, and praise. Do all you can to insure each other's success.

   "Two are better than one because they have a good return for their labor. For if either of them falls, the one will lift up his companion. But woe to the one who falls when there is not another to lift him up."   Ecclesiastes 4:9-10 (NASB)

3. Your minimum goal is to have each verse word perfect.
   a. Often your ability to quote a verse perfectly will give another person confidence in you, so that you can help him.
   b. It is mentally easier to retain a verse that has been learned perfectly.
   c. If you only know the content vaguely, or don't know the location of the verse, what you say will have less authority.
   d. Anything worth doing is worth doing well. "Whatever your task is, put your whole heart and soul into it, as into work done for the Lord and not merely for men" (Colossians 3:23, PH).
4. When listening, signal the quoter when he makes a mistake, but give him verbal help only when asked.

5. After the quoter has corrected his mistake, have him repeat the verse word-perfect before going on to another verse.

6. Review your verses with someone using the same translation.

Tyranny of the Urgent
Charles E. Hummel

Have you ever wished for a thirty-hour day? Surely this extra time would relieve the tremendous pressure under which we live. Our lives leave a trail of unfinished tasks. Unanswered letters, unvisited friends, unwritten articles, and unread books haunt quiet moments when we stop to evaluate. We desperately need relief.

But would a thirty-hour day really solve the problem? Wouldn't we soon be just as frustrated as we are now with our twenty-four allotment? A mother's work is never finished, and neither is that of any student, teacher, minister, or anyone else we know. Nor will the passage of time help us catch up. Children grow in number and age to require more of our time. Greater experience in profession and church brings more exacting assignments. So we find ourselves working more and enjoying it less.

JUMBLED PRIORITIES . . . ?

When we stop to evaluate, we realize that our dilemma goes deeper than shortage of time; it is basically the problem of priorities. Hard work does not hurt us. We all know what it is to go full speed for long hours, totally involved in an important task. The resulting weariness is matched by a sense of achievement and joy. Not hard work, but doubt and misgiving produce anxiety as we review a month or year and become oppressed by the pile of unfinished tasks. We sense uneasily that we may have failed to do the important. The winds of other people's demands have driven us onto a reef of frustration. We confess, quite apart from our sins, "We have left undone those things which we ought to have done; and we have done those things which we ought not to have done."

Several years ago an experienced cottonmill manager said to me, "Your greatest danger is letting the urgent things crowd out the important." He didn't realize how hard his maxim hit. It often returns to haunt and rebuke me by raising the critical problem of priorities.

We live in constant tension between the urgent and the important. The problem is that the important task rarely must be done today or even this week. Extra hours of prayer and Bible study, a visit with that non-Christian friend, careful study of an important book: these projects can wait. But the urgent tasks call for instant action—endless demands pressure every hour and day.

A man's home is no longer his castle; it is no longer a place away from urgent tasks because the telephone breaches the walls with imperious demands. The momentary appeal of these tasks seems irresistible and important, and they devour our energy. But in the light of time's perspective their deceptive prominence fades; with a sense of loss we recall the important task pushed aside. We realize we've become slaves to the tyranny of the urgent.

CAN YOU ESCAPE . . . ?

Is there any escape from this pattern of living? The answer lies in the life of our Lord. On the night before He died, Jesus made an astonishing claim. In the great prayer of John 17 He said, "I have finished the work which Thou gavest Me to do" (verse 4).

How could Jesus use the word "finished"? His three-year ministry seemed all too short. A prostitute at Simon's banquet had found forgiveness and a new life, but many others still walked the street without forgiveness and a new life. For every ten withered muscles that had flexed into health, a hundred remained impotent. Yet on that last night, with many useful tasks undone and urgent human needs unmet, the Lord had peace; He knew He had finished God's work.

The Gospel records show that Jesus worked hard. After describing a busy day Mark writes,

"That evening, at sundown, they brought to Him all who were sick or possessed with demons. And the whole city was gathered about the door. And He healed many who were sick with various diseases, and cast out many demons" (1:32-34).

On another occasion the demand of the ill and maimed caused Him to miss supper and to work so late that His disciples thought He was beside Himself (Mark 3:21). One day after a strenuous teaching session, Jesus and His disciples went out in a boat. Even a storm didn't awaken Him (Mark 4:37-38). What a picture of exhaustion.

Yet His life was never feverish; He had time for people. He could spend hours talking to one person, such as the Samaritan woman at the well. His life showed a wonderful balance, a sense of timing. When His brothers wanted Him to go to Judea, He replied, "My time has not yet come" (John 7:6). Jesus did not ruin His gifts by haste. In *The Discipline and Culture of the Spiritual Life,* A. E. Whiteham observes: "Here in this Man is adequate purpose . . . inward rest, that gives an air of leisure to His crowded life: above all there is in this Man a secret and a power of dealing with the waste-products of life, the waste of pain, disappointment, enmity, death—turning to divine uses the abuses of man, transforming arid places of pain to fruitfulness, triumphing at last in death, and making a short life of thirty years or so, abruptly cut off, to be a 'finished' life. We cannot admire the poise and beauty of this human life, and then ignore the things that made it."

WAIT FOR INSTRUCTIONS . . .

What was the secret of Jesus' work? We find a clue following Mark's account of Jesus' busy day. Mark observes that ". . . in the morning, a great while before day, He rose and went out to a lonely place, and there He prayed" (Mark 1:35). Here is the secret of Jesus' life and work for God: *He prayerfully waited for His Father's instructions* and for the strength to follow them. Jesus had no divinely-drawn blueprint; He discerned the Father's will day by day in a life of prayer. By this means He warded off the urgent and accomplished the important.

Lazarus's death illustrates this principle. What could have been more important than the urgent message from Mary and Martha, "Lord, he whom You love is ill" (John 11:3)? John records the Lord's response in these paradoxical words: "Now Jesus loved Martha and her sister and Lazarus. So when He heard that he was ill, He stayed two days longer in the place where He was" (verses 5-6). What was the urgent need? Obviously to prevent the death of this beloved brother. But the important thing from God's point of view was to raise Lazarus from the dead. So Lazarus was allowed to die. Later Jesus revived him as a sign of His magnificent claim, "I am the resurrection and the life; he who believes in Me though he die, yet shall he live" (verse 25).

We may wonder why our Lord's ministry was so short, why it could not have lasted another five or ten years, why so many wretched sufferers were left in their misery. Scripture gives no answer to these questions, and we leave them in the mystery of God's purposes. But we do know that Jesus' prayerful waiting for God's instructions freed Him from the tyranny of the urgent. It gave Him a sense of direction, set a steady pace, and enabled Him to do every task *God* assigned. And on the last night He could say, "I have finished the work which Thou gavest Me to do."

DEPENDENCE MAKES YOU FREE . . .

Freedom from the tyranny of the urgent is found in the example and promise of our Lord. At the end of a vigorous debate with the Pharisees in Jerusalem, Jesus said to those who believed in Him: "If you continue in My Word, you are truly My disciples, and you will know the truth, and the truth will make you free. . . . Truly, truly, I say to you, everyone who commits sin is a slave to sin. . . . So if the Son makes you free, you will be free indeed" (John 8:31-36).

Many of us have experienced Christ's deliverance from the penalty of sin. Are we letting Him free us from the tyranny of the urgent? He points the way: "If you *continue* in My Word." This is the way to freedom. Through prayerful meditation on God's Word we gain His perspective.

P. T. Forsyth once said, "The worst sin is prayerlessness." We usually think of murder, adultery, or theft as among the worst. But the root of all sin is self-sufficiency—independence from God. When we fail to wait prayerfully for God's guidance and strength we are saying, with our actions if not our lips, that we do not need Him. How much of our service is characterized by "going it alone"?

The opposite of such independence is prayer in which we acknowledge our need of God's instruction and supply. Concerning a dependent relationship with God, Donald Baillie says: "Jesus lived His life in complete dependence upon God, as we all ought to live our lives. But such dependence does not destroy human personality. Man is never so truly and fully personal as when he is living in complete dependence upon God. This is how personality comes into its own. This is humanity at its most personal."

Prayerful waiting on God is indispensable to effective service. Like the time-out in a football game, it enables us to catch our breath and fix new strategy. As we wait for directions, the Lord frees us from the tyranny of the urgent. He shows us the truth about Himself, ourselves, and our tasks. He impresses on our minds the assignments He wants us to undertake. The need itself is not the call; the call must come from the God who knows our limitations. "The Lord pities those who fear Him. For He knows our frame; He remembers that we are dust" (Psalm 103:13-14). It is not God who loads us until we bend or crack with an ulcer, nervous breakdown, heart attack, or stroke. These come from our inner compulsions coupled with the pressure of circumstances.

EVALUATE

The modern businessman recognizes this principle of taking time out for evaluation. When Greenwalt was president of DuPont, he said, "One minute spent in planning saves three or four minutes in execution." Many salesmen have revolutionized their business and multiplied their profits by setting aside Friday afternoon to plan carefully the major activities for the coming week. If an executive is too busy to stop and plan, he may find himself replaced by another man who takes time to plan. If the Christian is too busy to stop, take spiritual inventory, and receive his assignments from God, he becomes a slave to the tyranny of the urgent. He

may work day and night to achieve much that seems significant to himself and others, but he will not finish the work God has for him to do.

A quiet time of meditation and prayer at the start of the day refocuses our relationship with God. Recommit yourself to His will as you think of the hours that follow. In these unhurried moments list in order of priority the tasks to be done, taking into account commitments already made. A competent general always draws up his battle plan before he engages the enemy; he does not postpone basic decisions until the firing starts. But he is also prepared to change his plans if an emergency demands it. So try to implement the plans you have made before the day's battle against the clock begins. But be open to any emergency interruption or unexpected person who may call.

You may also find it necessary to resist the temptation to accept an engagement when the invitation first comes over the telephone. No matter how clear the calendar may look at the moment, ask for a day or two to pray for guidance before committing yourself. Surprisingly the engagement often appears less imperative after the pleading voice has become silent. If you can withstand the urgency of the initial moment, you will be in a better position to weigh the cost and discern whether the task is God's will for you.

In addition to your daily quiet time, set aside one hour a week for spiritual inventory. Write an evaluation of the past, record anything God may be teaching you, and plan objectives for the future. Also try to reserve most of one day each month for a similar inventory of longer range. Often you will fail. Ironically, the busier you get the more you need this time of inventory, but the less you seem to be able to take it. You become like the fanatic, who, when unsure of his direction, doubles his speed. And frenetic service for God can become an escape from God. But when you prayerfully take inventory and plan your days, it provides fresh perspective on your work.

CONTINUE THE EFFORT . . .

Over the years the greatest continuing struggle in the Christian life is the effort to make adequate time for daily waiting on God, weekly inventory, and monthly planning. Since this time for receiving marching orders is so important, Satan will do everything he can to squeeze it out. Yet we know from experience that only by this means can we escape the tyranny of the urgent. This is how Jesus succeeded. He did not finish all the urgent tasks in Palestine or all the things He would have liked to do, but He did finish the work which God gave Him to do. The only alternative to frustration is to be sure that we are doing what God wants. Nothing substitutes for knowing that this day, this hour, in this place we are doing the will of the Father. Then and only then can we think of all the other unfinished tasks with equanimity and leave them with God.

Sometime ago Simba bullets killed a young man, Dr. Paul Carlson. In the providence of God his life's work was finished. Most of us will live longer and die more quietly, but when the end comes, what could give us greater joy than being sure that we have finished the work *God* gave us to do? The grace of our Lord Jesus Christ makes this fulfillment possible. He has promised deliverance from sin and the power to serve God in the tasks of His choice. The way is clear. If we continue in the Word of our Lord, we are truly His disciples. And He will free us from the tyranny of the urgent, free us to do the important, which is the will of God.

A Discussion of Tyranny of the Urgent

"It seems to me that perfection of means and confusion of goals seem to characterize our age."
—Albert Einstein

"The good is often the enemy of the best."
—Unknown

1. Define the word *urgent* as used in *Tyranny of the Urgent.*

   _____

   _____

2. Define the word *important* as used in *Tyranny of the Urgent.*

   _____

   _____

3. In the space below, jot down the thoughts that most impressed you from your reading of *Tyranny of the Urgent.*

   _____

   _____

   _____

4. During your discussion of this material, jot down the best thoughts shared by others.

   _____

   _____

   _____

5. Although the assignments in this course are not very long, they will take time to complete. It is important to plan time for each of your course activities so that they are assigned proper priority and not left to the last minute to complete. Pray and think about your weekly schedule and indicate below when you plan to do the assignments required for the course.

Reading and Marking Daily   Time _____ Place _____

Bible Study/Other Assignments Day(s) _____ Time _____ Place _____

Scripture Memory Daily   Times _____ Places _____

(Remember to buy up precious wasted minutes by carrying your verses in your verse pack so that you can memorize and review in your spare moments.)

CHRIST THE CENTER

Jesus Christ is Savior and Lord!

   William Barclay has pointed out that "of all the titles of Jesus the title Lord became by far the most commonly used, widespread, and theologically important. It would hardly be going too far to say that the word Lord became a synonym for the name Jesus." This sometimes neglected aspect of the Christian experience must be carefully considered by all men and women who want to be His disciples.

THINK ABOUT: What are some indicators of what is central in our lives?

THE LORD JESUS CHRIST

1. Titles reveal important information about the person to whom they refer. What are Jesus Christ's titles in the following verses?

John 13:13 _____

Acts 2:36 _____

Revelation 19:16 _____

Summarize what these titles reveal about Jesus Christ:

_____

_____

_____

_____

2. List what you learned about Christ from Colossians 1:15-20.

_____

_____

_____

_____

_____

In light of who Christ is, what position has the Father given Him? (Verse 18)

_____

_____

_____

Christ should have the same place in our hearts that He holds in the universe.

3. Examine Philippians 2:9-11.

   a. How has God exalted Jesus Christ?

   _____

   _____

   b. How will every person exalt Him?

   _____

   _____

4. Read 1 Corinthians 6:19-20.

   a. How did you become God's possession?

   _____

   _____

   b. Therefore, what should you do?

   _____

   _____

   _____

Jesus Christ, Lord of lords, has always existed and always will. Not all people allow Him to be the center of their lives, but that does not alter the fact of His lordship. All will someday acknowledge Christ as Lord, but the privilege of acknowledging His lordship and allowing him to be the center of our lives is possible now. Allow Christ to be the Lord of your life—by a decision followed by daily practice.

ACKNOWLEDGE HIS LORDSHIP

> Christ is present in all Christians;
> Christ is prominent in some Christians;
> But in only a few Christians is Christ preeminent.

5. What are we commanded to do in Romans 12:1?

_____

Why should you do this?

_____   _____

_____

6. There are many reasons why people are reluctant to give Christ access to every area in their lives. Check any of the sentences below which may apply to you.

a. I generally think or feel that . . .

_____ Jesus doesn't really understand my problems.

_____ He may want me to do something I can't.

_____ He may want me to enter a career which I could not enjoy.

_____ He will prevent me from getting married.

_____ He will take away my enjoyment of possessions, hobbies, or friends.

_____ He can help me in the "big" things, but He doesn't care about the little things.

b. Are there any other fears which have prevented you from giving Christ access to every area of your life?

_____

_____

c. How does the statement in Jeremiah 29:11 dispel these fears?

_____

_____

_____

_____

"A clear and definite activity of the will is involved in recognizing His lordship, since He is to be Lord of all. By her 'I will' the bride at the marriage altar, ideally, forever enthrones her groom in her affections. In subsequent years she lives out in detail all that was implied in that momentary act of the will. A similar enthronement of Christ can result from a similar act of the will, for the same decision as enthrones Christ automatically dethrones self."
—J. Oswald Sanders

7. Good intentions don't guarantee good results. A good start does not ensure a strong finish—decision is only the beginning. Once you have acknowledged the lordship of Christ in your life, you will prove that He is Lord by submitting to Him hour by hour and obeying Him in the daily affairs of life. Some of these areas are represented in the following illustration.

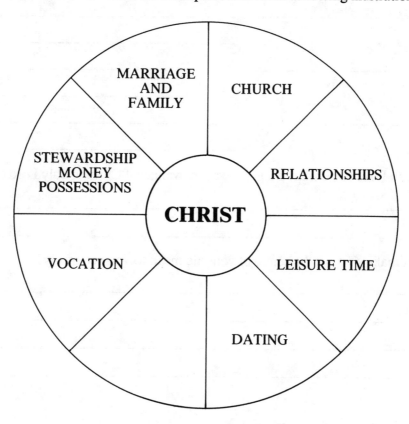

8. Take a few moments to evaluate your practice of the lordship of Jesus Christ.

   a. Over which of the above areas would you currently like to see Christ have more control?

   _____

   _____

   _____

   b. What are some specific changes you would like to see Christ help you make in these areas?

   _____

   _____

   _____

   _____

We should not be concerned about what we would do for the Lord if we only had more money, time, or education. Instead, we must decide what we will do with the things we have now. What really matters is whether Christ controls us.

9. What three things is the person who decides to follow Christ called to do? Luke 9:23

THE ACTION TO TAKE	WHAT THIS MEANS IN YOUR OWN WORDS

10. According to Luke 6:46, what is a good way to evaluate if Christ is truly Lord of your life?

_____

_____

11. What does making Christ the center of your life mean to you personally?

_____

_____

_____

_____

SUMMARY

Jesus Christ is declared to be Lord by God in the Scriptures. He is worthy to be Lord because of who He is, not merely because of what He has done.

Although Jesus Christ is Lord, He does not hold a preeminent place in the heart of every believer.

Various areas of a believer's life may not be subject to the control of Christ. The Christian should submit these areas to Christ and continue to recognize that Christ's control of his life is for his own welfare and joy.

How to Use My Personal Reading Record

My Personal Reading Record is a method for keeping track of where you are in reading the Bible. You will find it helpful and encouraging to use.

The books of the Bible are listed in the order in which they appear in Scripture. The Old and New Testaments are listed separately. The numbers which follow each book title are a list of the chapters in the book. For example, the Book of Romans has 16 chapters, so there are 16 numerals printed after it.

New Testament

Matthew	1	2	3	4	5	6	7	8	9	10	11	12	13	14	15	16	17	18	19	20
	21	22	23	24	25	26	27	28												
Mark	1	2	3	4	5	6	7	8	9	10	11	12	13	14	15	16				
Luke	1	2	3	4	5	6	7	8	9	10	11	12	13	14	15	16	17	18	19	20
	21	22	23	24																
John	1	2	3	4	5	6	7	8	9	10	11	12	13	14	15	16	17	18	19	20
	21																			
Acts	1	2	3	4	5	6	7	8	9	10	11	12	13	14	15	16	17	18	19	20
	21	22	23	24	25	26	27	28												
Romans	1	2	3	4	5	6	7	8	9	10	11	12	13	14	15	16				
1 Corinthians	1	2	3	4	5	6	7	8	9	10	11	12	13	14	15	16				
2 Corinthians	1	2	3	4	5	6	7	8	9	10	11	12	13							
Galatians	1	2	3	4	5	6														
Ephesians	1	2	3	4	5	6														
Philippians	1	2	3	4																

Let's say you spend some time today reading the first two chapters of Romans. After you have completed your reading, draw a diagonal line or an "X" through numerals 1 and 2.

Acts	1	2	3	4	5	6	7	8	9	10	11	12	13	14	15	16	17	18	19	20
	21	22	23	24	25	26	27	28												
Romans	X	X	3	4	5	6	7	8	9	10	11	12	13	14	15	16				
1 Corinthians	1	2	3	4	5	6	7	8	9	10	11	12	13	14	15	16				
2 Corinthians	1	2	3	4	5	6	7	8	9	10	11	12	13							

or

Acts	1	2	3	4	5	6	7	8	9	10	11	12	13	14	15	16	17	18	19	20
	21	22	23	24	25	26	27	28												
Romans	X	X	3	4	5	6	7	8	9	10	11	12	13	14	15	16				
1 Corinthians	1	2	3	4	5	6	7	8	9	10	11	12	13	14	15	16				

When you finish reading the book, you may want to record the date on which you completed it:

John	1	2	3	4	5	6	7	8	9	10	11	12	13	14	15	16	17	18	19	20
	21																			
Acts	1	2	3	4	5	6	7	8	9	10	11	12	13	14	15	16	17	18	19	20
	21	22	23	24	25	26	27	28												
Romans	X	X	X	X	X	X	X	X	X	X	X	X	X	X	X	X	May 25			
1 Corinthians	1	2	3	4	5	6	7	8	9	10	11	12	13	14	15	16				
2 Corinthians	1	2	3	4	5	6	7	8	9	10	11	12	13							
Galatians	1	2	3	4	5	6														

You will nearly always read one book all the way through before going on to another.

It is helpful to keep *My Personal Reading Record* in the Bible in which you are doing your reading. Be sure to fill in the record right after you finish your daily reading.

Keeping this record should motivate you as you see progress in your Bible reading.

ASSIGNMENT FOR SESSION 4:

1. Scripture Memory: Memorize the verse on "Assurance of Victory," 1 Corinthians 10:13.
2. Bible Reading: Continue your Bible reading and marking. Begin using *My Personal Reading Record* in conjunction with your Bible reading. Keep it up to date as you use it.
3. Bible Study: Complete the Bible Study, "Obedience" (pages 33-36).

Session 4

OUTLINE OF THIS SESSION:

1. Break into groups of two or three and review your memory verses:
    a. "Assurance of Salvation"—1 John 5:11-12
    b. "Assurance of Answered Prayer"—John 16:24
    c. "Assurance of Victory"—1 Corinthians 10:13
2. Share with the rest of the class what you have read and marked in your Bible this week.
3. Complete and discuss "Practical Suggestions on Prayer" (pages 30-33).
4. Discuss the Bible study, "Obedience" (pages 33-36).
5. Read the "Assignment for Session 5" (page 36).
6. Close the session in prayer.

Practical Suggestions on Prayer

THINK ABOUT:

"Prayer is not an attempt to change God's mind: Real prayer is communion with God: By it we express our trust in Him, seek to know His mind on the decisions of life, submit to His will, resist in His name the efforts of the devil to frustrate God's loving purposes in human lives."
—Leith Samuel

---

1. Prayer: An indispensable part of fellowship with God.

    a. Look up and summarize the following verses on fellowship with God.

    1 Corinthians 1:9 _____

    _____

    _____

    _____

    1 John 1:3 _____

    _____

    _____

    _____

b. What do you think are some keys to having effective fellowship with other people? List single words or short phrases.

_____

_____

_____

_____

Many of these same ingredients are essential to fellowship and communication between a person and God.

c. From your answers in "b" above, list two ingredients you feel are very important to fellowship and communication between a person and God.

1. _____

2. _____

d. What are the fewest elements you can have and still have fellowship with someone?

Answer: They talk to me as I _____ and I _____ to them as they listen.

2. An example of POOR COMMUNICATION with God.

The following diagram illustrates poor and ineffective communication with God during Bible reading and marking.

POOR COMMUNICATION

On the left we see the Christian listening as God speaks to him through the Bible. Then on the right we see the Christian praying after completing a time of Bible reading. But the topics of the prayer are unrelated to what God has just said to him. We would not be so rude as to ignore the statements of a human friend to pursue our own subjects of conversation. Yet we sometimes inadvertently do this to God. This is poor communication.

3. An example of EFFECTIVE COMMUNICATION WITH GOD.

The following diagram illustrates effective communication. As God impresses a truth to the Christian, he or she responds back to God in prayer. For example, praying for understanding, or asking for grace to apply a truth, or simply giving thanks or praise in response to a specific verse or passage. A person may then proceed to pray about various things not related to the Bible reading.

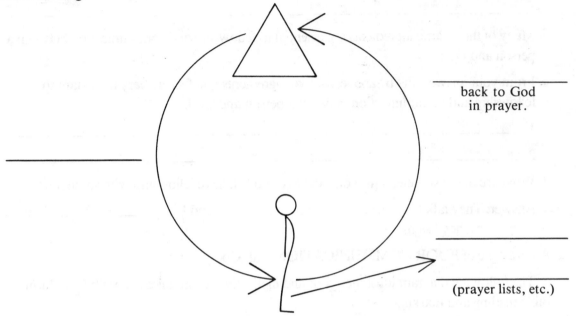

back to God
in prayer.

(prayer lists, etc.)

EFFECTIVE COMMUNICATION

The element that makes this second method so vital is the responding back to God in prayer. It can be done one of two ways:

a. You may comment back to God each time you mark something in your Bible.

b. You may complete your reading and marking and then go back to make a brief prayer comment about each thing you marked.

4. Prayer: Half of a communication process.

In our communication with God, there must be time for both listening and speaking. God primarily speaks to us through the Scriptures. We speak to God through prayer.
List observations about communication with God from the following two passages.

a. *"When Thou didst say,* 'Seek My Face,' my heart said to Thee, 'Thy face, O Lord, I shall seek.'"
                                                                —Psalm 27:8 (NASB)

_____

_____

_____

_____

b. "Let the morning bring me word of your unfailing love, for I have put my trust in you. . . .
Rescue me from my enemies, O LORD, for I hide myself in you. Teach me to do your will,
for you are my God; may your good Spirit lead me on level ground."

—Psalm 143:8-10

_____

_____

_____

_____

5. How the Trinity is involved in prayer: We pray to the Father, in the name of Christ, and
through the Holy Spirit.

Mark the box after you have read the verse(s) for each statement.

a. THE FATHER ☐

Our prayers should primarily be directed to the Father.

      Matthew 6:9   John 16:23   Ephesians 3:14

b. THE SON, JESUS CHRIST ☐

We come to the Father on the merits of Jesus Christ, that is, in His name; Christ is our access
to the Father.

      John 14:13,14   John 15:16   John 16:23,24

c. THE HOLY SPIRIT ☐

The Holy Spirit gives us guidance in what we should pray and interprets for the Father what
is on our hearts even when our words are poorly framed.

      Romans 8:26

"Groanings which cannot be uttered are often prayers which cannot be refused."

—C. H. Spurgeon

OBEDIENCE

At the moment you placed your faith in Jesus Christ as your Savior and Lord, a life of obedience
to God became an expected reality. The Holy Spirit set you free from sin and death (Romans 8:2),
and He came to live within you. The Holy Spirit enables you to live consistently with Jesus' values.

*". . . It is thus through His atoning death that the penalty of our sins may be forgiven;
whereas it is through His indwelling Spirit that the power of our sins may be broken."*

—John R. W. Stott

THINK ABOUT:
What are some similarities between the way children obey their parents and the way Christians obey God?

THE FOUNDATIONS OF OBEDIENCE

When you consider obedience to God, it is necessary to remember who He is and what He desires for you. How do you know what God desires for your life? The Bible is God's revelation of truth, and obedience to God's Word is obedience to God Himself.

1. After reflecting on John 14:15, 21, briefly state the relationship between loving God and obeying Him.

_____

_____

_____

_____

2. What did God require of Israel? Deuteronomy 10:12-13

_____

_____

_____

In what ways might obedience to God be profitable and "for your good", verse 13?

_____

_____

_____

"The key to usefulness, to revelation, and to a Holy Spirit-filled life is obedience to the Word of God."
                                                —Dr. John G. ("Jack") Mitchell

THE PRACTICE OF OBEDIENT LIVING

The obedient Christian still faces daily struggles with temptation and sin. How can you practice obedience and gain victory over sin? Important areas to consider are temptation, sin, confession, and victory.

3. Discover the source and causes of temptation in the following verses:

    a. Who is the tempter? Matthew 4:1-3 _____

    b. Who is never the source of temptation? James 1:13

    _____

c. What causes you to be drawn into temptation? James 1:14

_____

_____

(Lust is desire especially for what is forbidden.)

4. Using the following verses as a guide, write a brief definition of sin. Isaiah 53:6; James 4:17; 1 John 3:4

_____

_____

How does sin differ from temptation?

_____

_____

_____

While God offers victory and deliverance, men sin because they often neglect God's provision. Known but unconfessed sin grieves God. Although sin does not alter God's love, it does cause a break in fellowship with Him.

5. In Psalms 32:5, David prays and confesses his sin. Write this verse in your own words.

_____

_____

_____

_____

The practice of walking in victory can be pictured as follows:

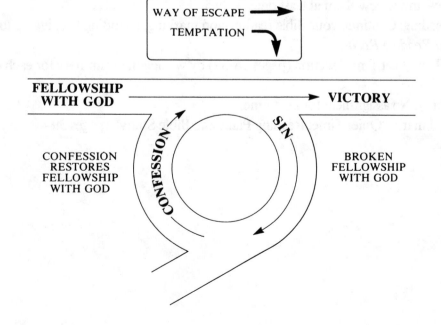

6. From Romans 6:11-14

   a. What should we do? (verses 11 and 13) _____

   b. What should we *not* do? (verses 12 and 13) _____

   _____

   _____

   c. What has God promised? (verse 14) _____

7. Identify and explain from James 4:7 what two steps will help you live a life of obedience?

_____

_____

"Live by the Spirit, and you will not gratify the desires of the sinful nature."

—Galatians 5:16

SUMMARY

Your obedience to God is based on God's love and concern for you. You obey Him because of who He is. But the life of obedience is also concerned with your own spiritual welfare. God reveals His standards through His Word. To the extent that you appropriate God's provision for victory, you can experience a life of obedience. You are not immune, however, from temptation. Sin does not negate God's love or your relationship with Him, but it does break your fellowship with Him. Confession of known sin restores fellowship with God once again.

ASSIGNMENT FOR SESSION 5:

1. Scripture Memory: No new verses are assigned for next session. Polish up the three passages you know and review them at least once daily.
2. Bible Reading: Continue your Bible reading and marking, including keeping up to date on *My Personal Reading Record*.
3. Fill in "The Quiet Time" section (pages 38-39) by writing in a summary for each of the eight verses.
4. Bible Study: No assignment for next time.
5. Read and mark, "Quiet Time, Reading Plans and Bible Study" (pages 39-40).

Session 5

OUTLINE OF THIS SESSION:

1. Break into groups of two or three and review your memory verses:
   a. "Assurance of Salvation"—1 John 5:11-12
   b. "Assurance of Answered Prayer"—John 16:24
   c. "Assurance of Victory"—1 Corinthians 10:13
2. Share with the rest of the class what you have read and marked in your Bible this week.
3. Read and discuss the "How" and "Why" of using the *Bible Reading Highlights Record* (pages 37-38). Locate the *Bible Reading Highlights Records* following page 115.
4. Discuss "The Quiet Time" (pages 38-39).
5. Discuss "Quiet Time, Reading Plans and Bible Study" (pages 39-40).
6. Discuss how to use your *Completion Record* (page 5).
7. Read the "Assignment for Session 6" (page 41).
8. Close the session in prayer.

How to Use Your Bible Reading Highlights Record

EACH DAY . . .

1. Do your daily Bible reading and marking.
2. Leaf back through what you have read and pick the one thought that is most interesting or helpful. It does not have to be an outstanding thought, just one that interests or helps you.
3. Fill in your *Bible Reading Highlights Record* this way:

   Translation—record the translation in which you are reading.

   Year—record the current year.

   O—refers to a checkpoint for recording Scripture memory review.

   Date—record the current date of your reading.

All I read today—record the reference for the day's reading, for example, Joshua 2-5, John 3.

Best thing I marked today—record the thought which you decide is the most interesting or helpful from the reading that day. For the Reference, put down the verse containing this thought, and for the Thought, paraphrase or quote it verbatim. Note this example:

Best thing I marked today: *Reference:* __John 3:16_____

Thought: __God loved the world so much that He gave His__
_____only Son to die for our sins._____

How it impressed me—what the phrase, sentence, or passage meant to you. For example:

How it impressed me: _I am struck with the idea that love isn't saying that you love someone, but love is giving up some of your own rights and conveniences. This, then, is a true expression of love!_

4. Write legibly. Keep your *Bible Reading Highlights Record* for future reference.

Why Use the Bible Reading Highlights Record

1. *It gives you one thought to reflect on each day.* Let's say you are impressed with an average of five things in your reading each day. If you isolate the best of the five, it gives you one thing to think about between readings. This allows God to use what He has been impressing on your mind to change your life. If you carry a vague assortment of ideas in your mind, God has less opportunity to change and enrich your life as a result of your reading.

2. *It may help you see trends in God's dealing with you.* With a record of major things God has been saying to you over a period of days or weeks, it is often possible to see a pattern. This may help you with planning about the future, understanding the past and present, or both.

3. *It gives you something specific to share with others.* Often if you are asked to give a devotional, teach a class, or deliver a message, this material which has already been so meaningful to you can be amplified or combined. It will be something about which God has spoken to you personally, not something from a book or manual that is from the life of another person (though some of these other materials can be helpful). Also, you will find other occasions to use these devotional thoughts to encourage and help other Christians.

4. *It helps to sharpen and organize your mind.* Learning to sift through your reading to determine what is most important will sharpen your mind to do the same thing in other areas such as Bible study, family decisions, and counseling.

5. *It stimulates consistency in your reading.* You may find, as others have, that having a definite form on which to write a thought each day will increase your consistency in reading. You will be less likely to miss a day when you realize there will be a blank space left on your record. This is not the best motive, perhaps, but it increases your consistency until you are properly motivated more often.

The Quiet Time

"The men who have most fully illustrated Christ in their characters, and have most powerfully affected the world for Him, have been men who spend so much time with God as to make it a notable feature in their lives. . . . To be little with God is to be little for God."

—E. M. Bounds

1. What is a quiet time?
   a. It is an unhurried time of Bible reading and prayer.
   b. It is the heart of your fellowship with God.
2. There are two major reasons for having a quiet time.
   a. FOR GROWTH AND NOURISHMENT. Food and proper nutrition are essential to healthy physical growth. In the same way, consistent intake of God's Word causes spiritual growth and good health. Summarize what the following verses say about spiritual growth and nourishment.

   1 Peter 2:2 _____

   Psalm 119:103 _____

   Jeremiah 15:16 _____

   Hebrews 5:12-14 _____

   b. FOR VITAL COMPANIONSHIP WITH JESUS CHRIST.

   "That we might accustom ourselves to a continual conversation with Him, with freedom and in simplicity. That we need only to recognize God intimately present with us."
   —Brother Lawrence

   Summarize what the following verses say about companionship with Jesus Christ.

   1 Corinthians 1:9 _____

   John 15:4 _____

   Micah 6:8 _____

   Psalm 16:11 _____

Quiet Time, Reading Plans, and Bible Study

1. READING
   There are several differences between Bible reading done during quiet time and the Bible reading done as part of a reading program or plan.
   a. Bible Reading: Quiet Time
   In the quiet time approach you have been learning in this course you read and mark only a chapter or two each day. You do not hurry. You are meeting a Person, not a habit. You expect God to impress you with something from the Scriptures that you personally need to hear that particular day. Over a period of several days or weeks you may detect patterns or a certain emphasis.

   During Bible study you will be more exacting and technical than you are in reading. When you read, you don't become involved in the details as much as in the overall theme of a chapter or book. Reading helps sharpen your familiarity with the characters and stories of both the Old and New Testaments.

Reading can be compared to flying over a city in an airplane or helicopter. We see the general layout of the city: major buildings, rivers, parks, and other landmarks. We miss much of the detail.

So, in the quiet time you are READING, MARKING, RESPONDING back to God in prayer, and WRITING something down.

This approach to Bible reading is meant to be fun and refreshing. It should be uplifting. Mark what impresses you and interests you—probably not some deep theological concept. Leave that for Bible study.

Spiritual edification is a major benefit of reading. As we read with an open heart to God, our thoughts, desires, and motivations are purified. Bible reading helps accomplish Paul's advice to us: "Do not conform any longer to the pattern of this world, but be transformed by the renewing of your mind [thinking process] . . ." (Romans 12:2). Reading God's Word is the very foundation of your quiet time.

b. Bible Reading: Reading Plans

Bible reading plans are designed to take a person through the Scriptures at a prescribed rate. A number of plans are designed to get you through the whole Bible in one calendar year. This requires reading three or four chapters per day.

Some reading programs border on being study programs. They are excellent but demand time and concentration. *Daily Walk* is a plan which provides a fairly rigorous schedule for each month and includes charts and commentary.

Most Bible reading plans involve more time and effort than the quiet time approach taught in *Growing Strong in God's Family.* They also may not personalize your time with God as well as your quiet time.

c. Having both a Quiet Time and a Reading Plan.

If you are not currently using a reading plan, you won't want to start one while you are taking *Growing Strong in God's Family.* It is better that you concentrate on enjoying your quiet time and being consistent in READING, MARKING, RESPONDING, and WRITING.

What if you are committed to a reading plan? You may decide to do some part of it during your quiet time and the rest at another time. You could elect to do your quiet time in one block of time and your reading plan at a separate time. Choose what fits your situation. Don't overload yourself. Follow a schedule that keeps reading enjoyable for you.

2. BIBLE STUDY

Whereas reading can give us an overview, Bible study opens up the details of a passage and how it relates to the whole teaching of Scripture. We compared reading to an aerial view of a city. Bible study is like driving through the city, learning street names and locating the supermarket, bank, and post office. We learn to be "at home" in the city—we know our way around. Bible study puts the teachings of Scripture together for us so we get a clear picture of specific truths. Bible study develops convictions.

Bible study is more time consuming than reading. We may be able to thoughtfully read through a chapter in 2-5 minutes. To study the same chapter may take us an hour or more. An advanced Bible student might profitably spend 5-10 hours on a chapter.

Bible reading and Bible study each play a distinctive role in sharpening and deepening our Christian lives and ministries.

ASSIGNMENT FOR SESSION 6:

1. Scripture Memory: Memorize the verse on "Assurance of Forgiveness," 1 John 1:9. Sharpen your review so your first four passages may be initialed on your *Completion Record* next week.
2. Quiet Time: Continue your Bible reading and marking. Pick a highlight from your reading each day and record it on your *Bible Reading Highlights Record.* Be sure to have your record with you next week so you can share something from it.
3. Bible Study: Complete the Bible Study "The Word" (pages 42-47).

Session 6

OUTLINE OF THIS SESSION:

1. Break into groups of two or three and review your memory verses:
   a. "Assurance of Salvation"—1 John 5:11-12
   b. "Assurance of Answered Prayer"—John 16:24
   c. "Assurance of Victory"—1 Corinthians 10:13
   d. "Assurance of Forgiveness"—1 John 1:9
2. Share some highlights from your reading, particularly those you have recorded on your *Bible Reading Highlights Record.*
3. Discuss the Bible study, "The Word" (pages 42-47).
4. Read and discuss the Evangelism Prayer List information on pages 47-48.
5. Read the "Assignment for Session 7" (page 48).
6. Close the session in prayer.

THE WORD

> **THINK ABOUT:**
> How would you respond to a skeptic's statement that the Bible is merely a book written by men and is no different from any other book?

The Bible is the most remarkable book ever written. The writing was done by about 40 men of several countries and many occupations. They wrote over a period of approximately 1,500 years and in three languages—Hebrew, Aramaic, and Greek. Yet the Bible has one great theme and central figure—Jesus Christ. All of this would be impossible unless the Bible had one supreme Author—and it does: The Holy Spirit of God.

GOD'S WORD: INSPIRED—RELIABLE—SUFFICIENT

1. How do the writers of Old Testament Scriptures attribute their words to God in the following passages?

   Nehemiah 9:13-14 _____

2 Samuel 23:1-3a _____

Jeremiah 1:6-9 _____

2. What conclusions about the reliability of Scripture can be drawn from the following New Testament passages:

1 Thessalonians 2:13 _____

2 Peter 1:20-21 _____

2 Peter 3:15-16 _____

Inspired comes from the Greek word meaning "God-breathed."

"The meaning, then, is not that God breathed into the writers, nor that He somehow breathed into the writings to give them their special character, but that what was written by men was breathed out by God. He spoke through them. They were His spokesmen."

—John R. W. Stott

3. How did Jesus use Scripture in the following situations?

a. In explaining the difference between true and false worship.

Mark 7:6-9 _____

_____

_____

_____

b. In answering a tough question about the resurrection.

Mark 12:24-27 _____

_____

_____

_____

c. In avoiding an argument with an insincere questioner.

Luke 10:25-28 _____

_____

_____

d. Jesus relied on God's Word for His life and ministry. What principles can you draw from Jesus' use of Scripture?

_____

_____

_____

4. 2 Timothy 3:16-17 is an excellent summary statement of the inspiration and sufficiency of God's Word.

    a. Identify and define four ways in which Scripture is of value to us.

       1. _____   _____

                                     _____

       2. _____   _____

                                     _____

       3. _____   _____

                                     _____

       4. _____   _____

                                     _____

    b. What is a major result of the Scriptures impacting our life? (verse 17)

_____

_____

GOD'S WORD IN YOUR LIFE

A sword is designed to be used skillfully in battle both as an offensive and a defensive weapon. God has equipped you with a tremendous instrument for spiritual battle: "the sword of the Spirit, which is the Word of God" (Ephesians 6:17). The Holy Spirit uses the Word of God to accomplish the work of God.

5. Examine Psalms 19:7-11 carefully. Use the following chart to aid you in your investigation. The Bible is referred to in various ways (law, testimony, precepts, etc.). Note below the Word's "characteristics", and what it will do for you.

VERSE	CHARACTERISTIC	WHAT IT WILL DO FOR ME
_____	_____	_____
_____	_____	_____
_____	_____	_____
_____	_____	_____

Which of the above characteristics is most important to you? Why?

_____

_____

_____

6. Analogy is a form which explains something by comparing it point by point with something similar. In the following verses, with what is God's Word compared? What is the function of these objects?

	OBJECT	FUNCTION
Jeremiah 23:29		
Matthew 4:4		
James 1:23-25		

7. Ezra is a good example of someone who felt a responsibility toward God's Word. What was his approach to Scripture? Ezra 7:10

_____

_____

_____

_____

8. From Joshua 1:8, briefly state the relationships between meditation, application, and success.

_____

_____

_____

_____

_____

_____

_____

9. How would you define meditation?

_____

_____

10. Using the material discussed in this chapter, state one important concept you studied this week.

_____

_____

_____

How can you incorporate this into your life to a greater degree?

_____

_____

_____

THE BIBLE AT A GLANCE (66 Books)

"The New is in the Old concealed;
The Old is in the New revealed."

OLD TESTAMENT (39 books)

HISTORY — 17 books

Law
1 Genesis
2 Exodus
3 Leviticus
4 Numbers
5 Deuteronomy

History and Government
1 Joshua
2 Judges
3 Ruth
4 1 Samuel
5 2 Samuel
6 1 Kings
7 2 Kings
8 1 Chronicles
9 2 Chronicles
10 Ezra
11 Nehemiah
12 Esther

POETRY — 5 books
1 Job
2 Psalms
3 Proverbs
4 Ecclesiastes
5 Song of Solomon

PROPHECY — 17 books

Major Prophets
1 Isaiah
2 Jeremiah
3 Lamentations
4 Ezekiel
5 Daniel

Minor Prophets
1 Hosea
2 Joel
3 Amos
4 Obadiah
5 Jonah
6 Micah
7 Nahum
8 Habakkuk
9 Zephaniah
10 Haggai
11 Zechariah
12 Malachi

NEW TESTAMENT (27 books)

HISTORY — 5 books

Gospels
1 Matthew
2 Mark
3 Luke
4 John
5 Acts

TEACHING — 21 books

Paul's Letters
1 Romans
2 1 Corinthians
3 2 Corinthians
4 Galatians
5 Ephesians
6 Philippians
7 Colossians
8 1 Thessalonians
9 2 Thessalonians
10 1 Timothy
11 2 Timothy
12 Titus
13 Philemon

General Letters
1 Hebrews
2 James
3 1 Peter
4 2 Peter
5 1 John
6 2 John
7 3 John
8 Jude

PROPHECY — 1 book
Revelation

The Old Testament looks forward to Christ's sacrifice on the Cross.

The New Testament is based on the work Christ finished on the Cross.

About 400 years between Testaments

God used 40 different men over a period of 1,500 years (about 1400 B.C. to A.D. 90) in writing the Bible— 2 Peter 1:20-21

SUMMARY

God has communicated to men and women through His Word—the Bible. The Bible is the final authority in all matters of faith and conduct. Through the Scriptures you can get to know God better, understand His desires for your life, and discover new truths about living for Him. God commands believers to let His Word dwell richly in them. So it is necessary to give yourself wholeheartedly to allowing God's Word to fill your life. God places great emphasis on the act of meditating on His Word, because effective meditation leads to understanding and personal application. Meditation and application will not only help you get into the Bible, but will also allow the Bible to get into you.

Why Have an Evangelism Prayer List

One of the most exciting events that can happen to you as a Christian is to see someone you know come to a saving knowledge of the Lord Jesus Christ. The situation that would make a person's conversion even more thrilling would be if you had been praying for that person.

In his book *Winning Ways,* LeRoy Eims makes the following statement, "If you want to see particular persons won to Christ, I suggest you put their names on a prayer list. Then pray for opportunities to share the Gospel with them, ask God to prepare their hearts and pray until God gives the promised answer." The Apostle Paul expressed his concern for his fellow Israelites in his letter to the Romans; "Brothers, my heart's desire and prayer to God for the Israelites is that they may be saved."

A key to seeing people come to Christ is to be specifically praying for them and "having them on your heart." An Evangelism Prayer list helps you do this.

Setting Up Your Evangelism Prayer List

1. Pray for wisdom in establishing your prayer list.
2. Try to list the names of between 5 and 10 non-Christians with whom you have contact. These could be neighbors, relatives, people at work, friends from school, and others. You can add other names to the list later as more people come to mind.
3. Use a 3 x 5 card to list these people and carry it in your Bible for easy reference. Put the card in your reading Bible as a marker. (Begin to pray regularly for these people and look for ways to develop relationships with them.)

Developing Contacts with Non-Christians

Many Christians find that they do not have any or have very few non-Christian friends. Some suggestions for developing contacts with non-Christians are:
1. Take the initiative to meet people, welcome new neighbors, and make friends. Be outside when

your neighbors are, attend school children's activities, participate in homeowners association meetings, etc.

2. Do things to deepen your relationships with your non-Christian friends. Join a club with them, go to social functions, develop hobbies or participate in sports together.

3. Be friendly and sociable. Try to leave the person with positive impressions.

Your goal is, at some point, to share your faith with them. Those people with whom you develop relationships will be far more inclined to listen to you. Pray about these activities, which are intermediate steps in a person coming to Christ.

ASSIGNMENT FOR SESSION 7:

1. Scripture Memory: Memorize the verses on "Assurance of Guidance," Proverbs 3:5-6.

2. Quiet Time: Continue your Bible reading and marking. Pick a highlight from your reading each day and record it on your *Bible Reading Highlights Record*.

3. Bible Study: There is no assignment for next time, but you may want to work ahead in your Bible study.

4. Evangelism Prayer List: Complete a list of 5-10 non-Christans on a 3x5 card and bring it with you for the next session.

5. Other:

   a. Come prepared to share what has impressed, helped or challenged you during this course.

   b. Study and be ready to discuss the material "Guide to Conversational Prayer" (pages 49-50).

   c. Review all previous material if you have not yet done so.

   d. Work on getting everything you can completed and ready to be signed on the *Completion Record.*

Session 7

OUTLINE OF THIS SESSION:

1. Break into groups of two or three and review all five *Beginning with Christ* verses.
2. Share some highlights from your reading, particularly those you have recorded on your *Bible Reading Highlights Record.*
3. Share what has impressed, helped, or challenged you during this course.
4. Discuss your Evangelism Prayer List.
5. Discuss "Guide to Conversational Prayer" (pages 49-50).
6. Have a brief time of conversational prayer on two or three topics.
7. Read the "Assignment for Session 8" (page 50).

Guide to Conversational Prayer

God desires your fellowship, and you can participate in a new dimension of communication with Him through conversational prayer. This type of prayer is designed to be used in a group. It is informal prayer where the objective is to speak conversationally with God from our hearts. Don't worry about impressing those who hear you. Be less concerned with the form of your prayer or with the specific words than with simply communicating with God.

Here are several guidelines:

1. *Start praying rather than sharing requests.* Much of your valuable prayer time can be taken up in sharing requests rather than praying. Usually the one with the burden for someone or something will be the one to initiate prayer about that person or thing.
2. *Pray about one topic at a time.* It is important to pray topically as much as possible. One person may pray about a sick friend, and the second person can stay on that topic by asking for strength for the family while the sick one recuperates. Then another may pray that the family's financial needs will be met during this lengthy illness. When there is a pause, someone may change the topic. For example, after a pause, a person may pray for help in having a consistent quiet time. Another may request that his quiet time be more meaningful. Another may pray that he will have the time to meditate on the Scripture he reads during his quiet time.

You want to keep from skipping around from topic to topic. You don't want a disjointed time, but a time when you can join in meaningful prayer in which you agree together concerning the requests at hand. From your heart you want to be praying along with the person who is praying aloud. He will then in turn be inaudibly praying along with you as you pray.

3. *Pray briefly.* Most individuals pray about two or three sentences at a time. By each person praying briefly, you each get to pray again sooner than if each person were to pray longer. This keeps each one alert, awake, and involved in what is being prayed. Pray for one subject at a time.

4. *Pray spontaneously, not in sequence.* Don't pray around the circle, but let each person pray for that which interests him. For example, if six subjects are prayed over in the conversational prayer time, you may have a vital interest in only three of them.

   Praying spontaneously does not mean praying thoughtlessly. While another is praying on the subject at hand, you have time for the Holy Spirit to confirm in your own heart what you would like to pray.

> Conversational Prayer Guidelines:
> 1. Don't share—pray.
> 2. One topic at a time.
> 3. Be brief.
> 4. Be spontaneous.

As a group begins conversational prayer there may need to be a few moments of silence while people quiet their hearts and collect their thoughts.

The group leader of any group will usually need to provide some direction on which the prayer time will be focused. Normally the focus of prayer should start with God and move toward request. This is usually best done by beginning with a period of praise and thanksgiving. The leader may suggest other areas in which the prayer should continue, such as needs within the group, and then later needs outside the group.

These areas of focus can vary significantly, the point is simply that people usually need direction regarding the parameters of the subjects for which the group is praying. It is more important to do a thorough job of praying for a few items than to scatter the prayers over too wide a range.

ASSIGNMENT FOR SESSION 8:
1. Scripture Memory: Work on completing the memory requirements for the course.
2. Quiet Time: Continue reading and marking in your Bible, using your *Bible Reading Highlights Record.*
3. Bible study: Complete the Bible study, "Prayer" (pages 51-55).

OUTLINE OF THIS SESSION:
1. Break into groups of two or three, review all five memory verses, and work on getting items initialed on your *Completion Record*.
2. Share at least one item from your *Bible Reading Highlights Record* with the rest of the class.
3. Discuss the Bible study, "Prayer" (pages 51-55).
4. Read the "Assignment for Session 9" (page 55).
5. Have a time of brief conversational prayer.

PRAYER

Communication is essential for a growing relationship. When you pray, the Holy Spirit helps you know what to say and how to say it. (Romans 8:26-27)

> "The great people of the earth today are the people who pray. I do not mean those who talk about prayer; not those who can explain about prayer; but I mean those people who take time and pray. They have not time. It must be taken from something else. This something else is important—very important and pressing, but still less important and less pressing than prayer."
> —S. D. Gordon

> "The Spirit links Himself with us in our praying and pours His supplication into our own. We may master the technique of prayer and understand its philosophy; we may have unlimited confidence in the veracity and validity of the promises concerning prayer. We may plead them earnestly. But if we ignore the part played by the Holy Spirit, we have failed to use the master key."
> —J. Oswald Sanders

THINK ABOUT:
Apart from salvation, what is the biggest thing for which you have ever prayed and the greatest answer you have ever received?

_____

_____

PRAYER—YOUR COMMUNICATION TO GOD

1. As a believer, you enjoy a relationship with Christ and have been given a special privilege. What is this privilege and why was it given? Hebrews 4:16

   _____

   _____

2. Because God is the believer's refuge, what are you told to do? Psalms 62:8

   _____

   _____

   _____

   What could hinder a person from doing this?

   _____

   _____

   _____

3. Different types of prayer are necessary to communicate the variety of thoughts you want to express. From the following verses, identify and define five types of prayer. Psalms 38:18, Hebrews 13:15, Luke 11:3, Ephesians 5:20, James 5:16

VERSE	TYPE	GIVE AN EXAMPLE
1. _____	Praise	_____
2. _____	Thanksgiving	_____
3. _____	Confession	_____
4. _____	Intercession	_____
5. _____	Supplication	_____

THE PRACTICE OF PRAYER

4. What conditions of prayer do you find in the following verses?

   Psalms 66:18 _____

   Matthew 21:22 _____

   John 15:7 _____

                    (Abide means to continue, dwell, endure)

   John 16:24 _____

   1 John 5:14-15 _____

   James 4:3 _____

Even when conditions are met, it sometimes appears as if God is not answering prayer. But remember that "No" and "Wait" are as much of an answer as "Yes."

5. Consider Jesus' pattern for prayer in Matthew 6:9-13.
   a. How does the prayer begin? Why is this important?

   _____

   _____

   _____

   b. Which requests are God-centered?

   _____

   _____

   c. Which requests are man-centered?

   _____

   _____

   d. In what specific ways can this pattern for praying help you pray?

   _____

   _____

   _____

   _____

6. From the following verses, list some of the categories of people for whom we should pray.
   Romans 10:1 _____

   1 Timothy 2:1-4 _____

   Matthew 9:37-38 _____

7. Using Paul's prayer as a guideline, list some requests you could pray for others and for yourself.
   Ephesians 3:14-21

   _____

   _____

   _____

   _____

   _____

   _____

   _____

Take a moment right now and use these requests to pray for someone you know. Write down the name of the person(s) for whom you prayed.

_____

"We should pray when we are in a praying mood, for it would be sinful to neglect so fair an opportunity. We should pray when we are not in a proper mood, for it would be dangerous to remain in so unhealthy a condition."   —Charles H. Spurgeon

Have you been using a prayer list? A list can help you remember things you might otherwise forget to pray about. It can include:

- your family
- your non-Christian friends and acqaintances
- your pastor and church
- missionaries and Christian workers you know

- those who oppose you
- governmental authorities
- your personal needs

8. Paul reveals a powerful key to freedom from worry and anxiety in Philippians 4:6-7.

   a. What are you to do? _____

   _____

   b. What is God's promise? _____

   c. In what area can you immediately begin to apply these truths?

   _____

   _____

   _____

Thou art coming to a King;
Large petitions with thee bring;
For His grace and power are such,
None can ever ask too much!
                                        —John Newton

9. Examine Luke 10:38-42. You can make several observations from this passage which relate to spending time with Jesus Christ.

   a. Contrast the activities of Mary and Martha.

   MARY   MARTHA

   _____   _____

   _____   _____

   _____   _____

   _____   _____

b. Which one did Jesus commend and why?

_____

_____

_____

c. Like Martha, you may be easily distracted by many things. What activities might distract you from listening to and conversing with God?

_____

_____

_____

d. What can you do to overcome these distractions?

_____

_____

_____

_____

"It is impossible for a believer, no matter what his experience, to keep right with God if he will not take the trouble to spend time with God. . . . Spend plenty of time with God; let other things go, but don't neglect Him."
                                                           —Oswald Chambers

SUMMARY

God has provided prayer as the means of communicating directly with Him. Christ, the great High Priest and Mediator, has made it possible for all Christians to come "boldly to the throne of grace." Prayer may take many forms of expression, some of which are adoration and praise, thanksgiving, confession, intercession, and supplication. Each of these enables you to draw closer to God. Since you have the potential of two-way communication with God, be careful not to neglect your time with Him. Regular times alone with God for the purpose of fellowship are vitally necessary.

ASSIGNMENT FOR SESSION 9:

1. Scripture Memory: Continue to review the *Beginning with Christ* verses daily.
2. Quiet Time: Continue reading and marking your Bible and using your *Bible Reading Highlights Record.*
3. Bible Study: Complete the Bible study, "Fellowship" (pages 64-68).
4. Other:
   a. Read the information on *The Wheel Illustation* (pages 56-63).
   b. Bring your Evangelism Prayer List to class. Come prepared to share problems and blessings in preparing and using it.

Session 9

OUTLINE OF THIS SESSION:

1. Break into groups of two or three, review all five memory verses, and work on getting items initialed on your *Completion Record.*
2. Share at least one item from your *Bible Reading Highlights Record* with the rest of the class.
3. Discuss *The Wheel Illustration* (pages 56-63).
4. Discuss your Evangelism Prayer List.
5. Discuss the Bible Study, "Fellowship" (pages 64-68).
6. Read the "Assignment for Session 10" (page 68).
7. Have a time of brief conversational prayer.

The Wheel Illustration

The Wheel Illustration depicts six of the crucially important components of a vital Christian life. Your Bible studies during this course cover each of these six topics.

Three important dimensions of the *Wheel* are:

1. **THE VOLITIONAL DIMENSION** (Relationship to the Will)
   THE HUB: CHRIST THE CENTER
   THE RIM: OBEDIENCE TO CHRIST

2. **THE VERTICAL DIMENSION** (Relationship to God)
   THE WORD SPOKE
   THE PRAYER SPOKE

3. **THE HORIZONTAL DIMENSION** (Relationship to Others)
   THE FELLOWSHIP SPOKE
   THE WITNESSING SPOKE

THE VOLITIONAL DIMENSION
(Relationship to the Will)
THE HUB: CHRIST THE CENTER

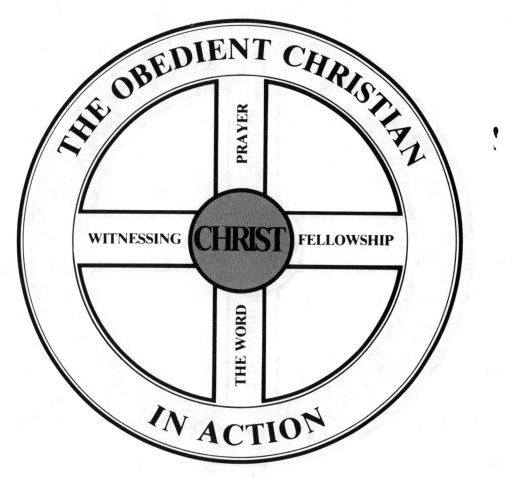

Memory verses:
2 Corinthians 5:17
Galatians 2:20

The act of making Christ central in your life, that is, giving Him the place of true lordship in your life, is really an act of your will. There should be a time in your life when you are willing to surrender totally to Christ's authority and lordship. This may be at conversion or after some months or even years.

It is true that lordship is a volitional matter, that is, a matter of your choice or your will. But as you pray and as others pray for you, God creates within you the desire to do what He wants you to do in order to express His lordship in your life.

"For it is God who works in you to will and to act according to his good purpose."
—Philippians 2:13

THE VOLITIONAL DIMENSION
(Relationship to the Will)
THE RIM: OBEDIENCE TO CHRIST

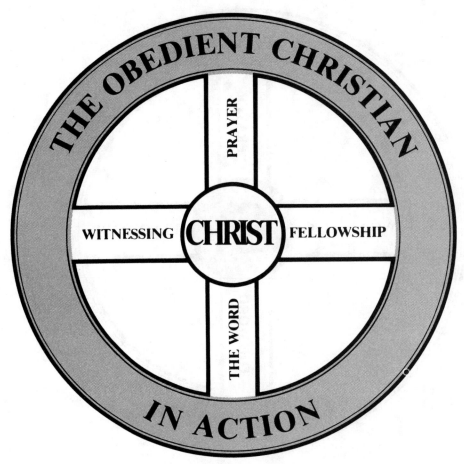

Memory verses:
Romans 12:1
John 14:21

When you are obedient to Christ and actively following God's leading, it shows in your outward life. People can see the evidences of your Christianity.

Some acts of obedience to God are more internal. They have to do with attitudes, habits, motives, sense of values, and day-to-day thoughts. These internal acts of obedience eventually surface in relationships with other people. The proof of your love for God is your demonstrated obedience to Him.

"But I gave them this command: Obey me, and I will be your God and you will be my people. Walk in all the ways I command you, that it may go well with you."

—Jeremiah 7:23

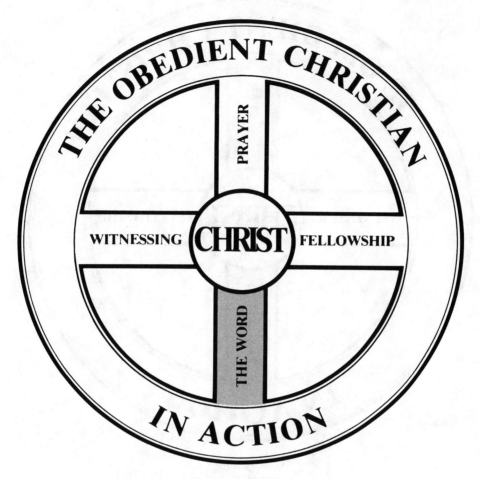

Memory verses:
2 Timothy 3:16
Joshua 1:8

In this illustration, the Word is the foundational spoke. In practice, this spoke is perhaps the most crucial element in a balanced Christian life. As God speaks to you through the Scriptures, you can see His principles for life and ministry, learn how to obey, and see Christ as worthy of your unqualified allegiance.

When a Christian has a vital personal intake of the Word of God, he is healthy and growing.

"All scripture is inspired by God and is useful for teaching the faith and correcting error, for re-setting the direction of a man's life and training him in good living. The scriptures are the comprehensive equipment of the man of God, and fit him fully for all branches of his work."
—2 Timothy 3:16-17, PH

THE VERTICAL DIMENSION
(Relationship to God)
THE PRAYER SPOKE

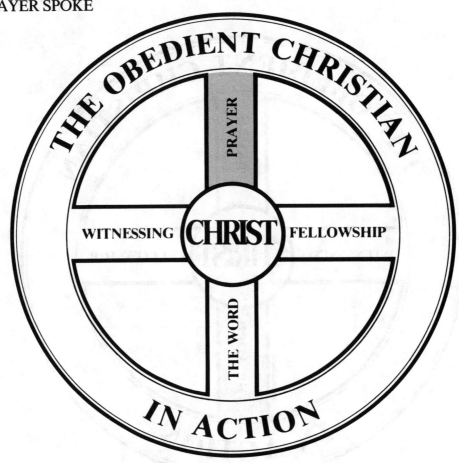

Memory verses:
John 15:7
Philippians 4:6-7

Prayer should be the natural overflow of meaningful time in the Scriptures. The act of prayer to God completes the fellowship and companionship element in your relationship with Him. Respond back to God in prayer after He speaks to you through His Word. In this manner, you share your heart with the One who longs for your companionship.

Prayer is how the power of God is unleashed. Personal battles and battles for others are won in prayer, and the cause of Christ is thus furthered.

"Call to Me and I will answer you and reveal to you great and mighty things which you do not know."   —Jeremiah 33:3, BERK

"You do not have, because you do not ask God."   —James 4:2b

THE HORIZONTAL DIMENSION
(Relationship to Others)
THE FELLOWSHIP SPOKE

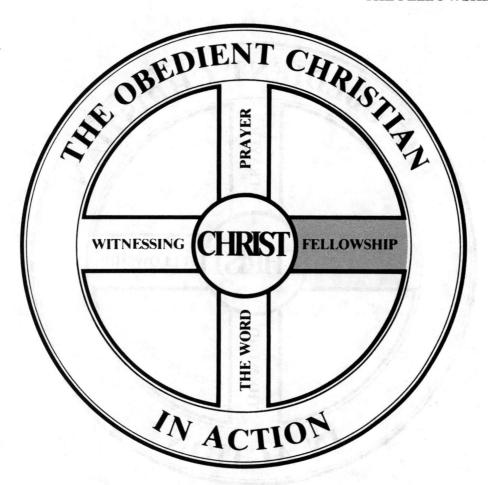

Memory verses:
1 John 1:3
Hebrews 10:24-25

Christians are neither higher nor lower than other people. Someone has said that "the ground is level at the foot of the cross." And all Christians have the wonderful privilege of being intimate members of God's family.

God has directed Christians to fellowship with other Christians. You are to learn from others and to encourage one another. There is a certain chemistry that takes place as Christians get together to build each other up. This cannot be accomplished if you operate independently and are isolated from other Christians.

"From him the whole body, joined and held together by every supporting ligament, grows and builds itself up in love, as each part does its work." —Ephesians 4:16

THE HORIZONTAL DIMENSION
(Relationship to Others)
THE WITNESSING SPOKE

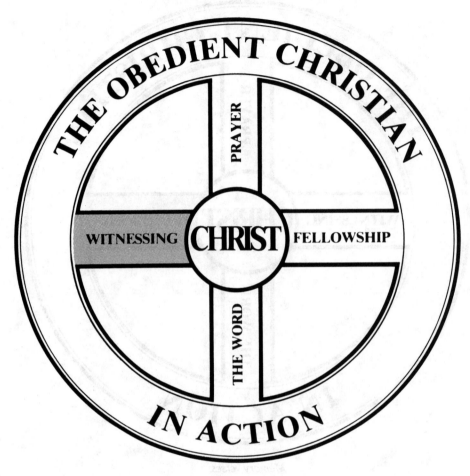

Memory verses:
Matthew 4:19
Romans 1:16

    The natural overflow of a rich and vibrant life in Christ should be sharing with others how they too can have this life. Your devotional life, extended times of prayer, and prompt obedience to God will give your life an attractiveness which adds credibility to your words.

    Effective witnessing also involves skills. Skills can be learned and sharpened. You will become a sharpened instrument in God's hand as you receive training and gain experience in witnessing.

> *"But you will receive power when the Holy Spirit comes on you; and you will be my witnesses in Jerusalem, and in all Judea and Samaria, and to the ends of the earth."*
>
>   —Acts 1:8

THE COMPOSITE
(The Wheel as a Whole)

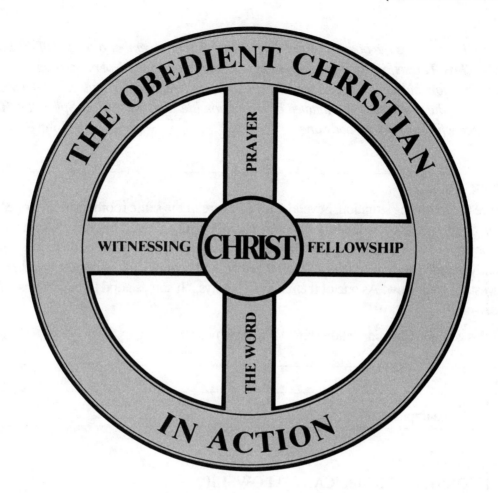

Usually "either/or" thinking is not reliable. Usually life is "both/and." It is not *either* fellowship *or* witnessing; it is not *either* prayer *or* an intake of the Word. A balanced Christian life should be *all* of these. This balance should be the desire of every Christian.

Develop your strengths and trust God to use them to the fullest extent. Also work on your deficiencies and inadequacies, trusting the Holy Spirit to continue to renovate you.

The Wheel is a good checklist for evaluating growth and balance in your spiritual life. Over the months and years you should see a continual development and strengthening of your spiritual life in all these areas.

> *"And they persevered in the apostles' teaching and in fellowship, in the breaking of bread and in prayer . . . praising God with happy and sincere hearts, and enjoying the good will of all the people, while daily the Lord added to the group those who were being saved."*
> —Acts 2:42-47, BERK

FELLOWSHIP

"The Church . . . is the body of Christ. Every Christian is a member or organ of the body, while Christ Himself is the Head, controlling the body's activities. Not every organ has the same function, but each is necessary for the maximum health and usefulness of the body. Moreover, the whole body is animated by a common life. This is the Holy Spirit. It is His presence which makes the body one."
　　　　　　　　　　　　　　　　　　　　　　　　　　　　　　　　—John R. W. Stott

THINK ABOUT:

Picture the following situation. Several Christians are in the same room drinking coffee and eating doughnuts as they discuss last week's championship game. The conversation moves to the subject of "which animal makes the best household pet." Then one of them tells a joke he recently heard. They enjoy a good laugh together, and begin to talk about the weather forecast for tomorrow. As one of them leaves, he says, "It sure is good to have Christian fellowship!"

a. Is this genuine Christian fellowship? Why or why not?

_____

_____

b. Could it be improved? How? _____

WHAT CONSTITUTES BIBLICAL FELLOWSHIP?

1. God uses the analogy of a body to describe the relationship of believers with one another and with Christ. Who is the Head of the body? Why? Colossians 1:18

_____

_____

_____

_____

2. "Fellowship" is derived from the Greek word koinonia, which means "sharing in common". God has given you much to share. As you examine the verses below, determine what you can share with others. In addition, give one practical way to share it.

　　　　　　　　　　　　　　　　WHAT TO SHARE　　　　　　**A WAY TO SHARE**

1 John 4:11,21　　　　　_____　　_____

　　　　　　　　　　　　　　　　　　　　　　　　　　　　　　_____

Galatians 6:2 _____   _____
                                         _____

2 Corinthians 8:13-15 _____   _____
                                         _____

1 Thessalonians 2:8 _____   _____
                                         _____

James 5:16 _____   _____
                                         _____

(Spiritual means Spirit-controlled)

Sharing involves giving and receiving. Both are integral parts of meaningful fellowship.

3. Christians fellowship together on the basis of the fact that their sins are forgiven. The forgiveness we have experienced should affect how we respond to others when offenses are involved.

   a. What do we learn about broken fellowship from the following two passages? Matthew 5:23-24, Matthew 18:15,35

      _____

      _____

      _____

   b. Why should reconciliation take priority over worship? (Reference Matthew 5:23-24)

      _____

      _____

   Christians can honestly share their lives. You don't have to pretend to be something you are not.

   "The Church is the only fellowship in the world where the one requirement for membership is the unworthiness of the candidate."   —Robert B. Munger

4. Identify some benefits of fellowship from the following passages.

   Proverbs 27:17 _____

   Ecclesiastes 4:9-10 _____

   Hebrews 3:13 _____

   Which one could you best help provide for another Christian?

   _____

   _____

Which benefit do you usually receive from other Christians?

_____

_____

FELLOWSHIP IN THE BODY OF CHRIST

5. Each believer is given different but important responsibilities in this spiritual body, the Church. Read 1 Corinthians 12:14-27.

   a. Who gave the members their various functions? Verse 18

   _____

   b. What is His desire? Verse 25

   _____

   c. What attitudes can lead to disharmony in the body? Verses 15,16,21

   _____

   _____

   _____

   d. Why are there no unnecessary functions (members) in the body? Verses 20-22

   _____

   _____

6. Think of what happens when you hit your finger with a hammer. How does this affect the entire body?

   _____

   _____

   How can this illustration relate to the spiritual body? 1 Corinthians 12:26

   _____

   _____

   _____

7. The body works together as one unit, yet it has many specialized organs which perform diverse functions. Summarize in a couple of sentences how both unity and diversity can exist together in the Body.

   _____

   _____

   _____

   _____

8. Examine your attitudes toward other Christians. Is there someone with whom you find it difficult to relate as another member of Christ's body? Why?

_____

_____

_____

What steps can you take to bring harmony to your relationship with this individual?

_____

_____

_____

_____

"How good and pleasant it is when brothers live together in unity!"   —Psalm 133:1

THE CHURCH—MANIFESTED LOCALLY

9. What activities of the local church in Jerusalem are mentioned in Acts 2:41-42?

_____

_____

_____

Three distinguishing marks of the Early Church were
(1) GENEROSITY   (2) PRAYER   (3) POWER

10. Read Ephesians 4:11-13. What is the responsibility of apostles, prophets, evangelists, pastors, and teachers?

_____

_____

What should be the end result of this process? Ephesians 4:13

_____

_____

_____

_____

11. What are some responsibilities we have to one another in a fellowship of believers?

Ephesians 5:21 _____

Colossians 3:16 _____

1 Thessalonians 4:18 _____

1 Thessalonians 5:11 _____

Hebrews 10:24-25 _____

James 5:16 _____

In which of these responsibilities do you think you could best contribute to meeting needs among other believers? Explain briefly.

_____

_____

12. Review your answers in this Bible study. List two reasons why you believe fellowship is indispensable.

_____

_____

_____

_____

"So we, numerous as we are, are one body in Christ, the Messiah, and individually we are parts one of another—mutually dependent on one another."   —Romans 12:5

SUMMARY

Genuine fellowship is based on the concept of giving to and receiving from other Christians. You can share with others whatever God has given you—forgiveness, possessions, love, His Word, and many other things. God gives fellowship for the purpose of mutual encouragement and growth. He wants Christians to live in unity and harmony with one another. To help us understand how believers are related, God uses the analogy of the body. Jesus Christ is the Head of the Body, which is comprised of all believers. All Christians throughout the world belong to Christ's Body, but it is important for you to recognize how God wants you to be related to a smaller, specific group of believers. This smaller group is for the purpose of instruction, sharing, worship, and service. God has given spiritual leaders to help you mature in Christ and to become effective in the ministry.

ASSIGNMENT FOR SESSION 10:

1. Quiet Time: Continue reading and marking in your Bible and using your *Bible Reading Highlights Record.*
2. Other: Complete "A Personal Evaluation of the Wheel in My Life" (page 69). Come with points 1 and 2 completed, and at least one item under point 3.
3. Scripture Memory: List at least five reasons why a person would memorize Scripture in Part 1 of "Why Memorize Scripture" (page 70). Number each one. You will be adding to your list as others share what they have written. Fill in Part 2 and be ready to discuss it.
4. Bible Study: Complete the Bible study "Witness" (pages 71-73).
5. Other: Work on getting anything remaining completed so that you can get it signed off on your *Completion Record.*

Session 10

OUTLINE OF THIS SESSION:
1. Break into groups of two or three, review all five memory verses, and work on getting items initialed on your *Completion Record.*
2. Share at least one item from your *Bible Reading Highlights Record* with the rest of the class.
3. Discuss "A Personnel Evaluation of the Wheel in My Life" (page 69).
4. Discuss "Why Memorize Scripture" (page 70).
5. Check to see that all items on your *Completion Record* have been initialed and that your leader signs the "Graduated from *Growing Strong in God's Family*".
6. Discuss the Bible study, "Witness" (pages 71-73).
7. Read aloud "Keep Growing" page 74.
8. Have a time of brief conversational prayer.

A Personal Evaluation of the Wheel in My Life

1. I feel I am strongest in _____

2. I feel I am weakest in _____

3. Personal observations or questions: _____

_____

_____

_____

_____

_____

4. Comments from others: _____

_____

_____

_____

_____

_____

Why Memorize Scripture

Part 1—List some of the reasons why a person would *memorize* Scripture:

_____

_____

_____

_____

_____

_____

_____

Part 2—

  a. The primary personal benefit I expect from Scripture memory is (you may list two or three other benefits that strongly motivate you to continue Scripture memory):

_____

_____

_____

_____

_____

_____

_____

_____

_____

_____

  b. One or two attitudes or influences which could hinder my success in meaningful Scripture memory are:

_____

_____

_____

_____

_____

_____

_____

_____

WITNESS

"It is the Holy Spirit, not we, who converts an individual. We, the privileged ambassadors of Jesus Christ, can communicate a verbal message; we can demonstrate through our personality and life what the grace of Jesus Christ can accomplish. . . . But let us never naively think that we have converted a soul and brought him to Jesus Christ. . . . No one calls Jesus Lord except by the Holy Spirit."

—Paul Little

THINK ABOUT:
What parallels do you see between fishing for fish and "fishing for people?"

THE CHALLENGE

1. What is the cause and effect relationship in Jesus' statement found in Matthew 4:19?

   _____

   _____

   _____

2. In Mark 5:19, you'll discover Jesus' desire concerning a man He has healed.

   a. Where did He send him? _____

   b. What did He tell him to do? _____

   _____

   c. Why do you suppose Jesus gave these particular instructions?

   _____

   _____

   d. What application can we draw from this account?

   _____

   _____

   _____

3. Carefully examine 2 Corinthians 5:9-14. In this section Paul lists several motivations and reasons for witnessing for Christ.

   a. List those you discover.

   Verse 9 _____

   Verse 10 _____

Verse 11 _____

Verse 14 _____

b. Using external resources (dictionaries, encyclopedias, etc.), define and describe "an ambassador's function".

_____

_____

_____

_____

_____

PRESENTING THE MESSAGE

4. What is the Gospel as stated in 1 Corinthians 15:1-4?

_____

_____

_____

_____

5. Read 1 Corinthians 15:12-19, and list several reasons why the resurrection is an essential part of the Gospel message.

_____

_____

_____

6. What attitudes did Paul have about sharing the Gospel?

Acts 20:24 _____

_____

Romans 1:15-16 _____

_____

Mark an "X" on the line below where you feel you are now in your attitude about sharing the gospel?

       Ashamed of _____ Eager to preach
       the Gospel   the Gospel

THE MESSENGER
"God hasn't engaged many of us to be lawyers, but He has summoned all of us as witnesses."
                                                    —Anonymous

Witnessing is not merely an activity—it is a way of life. Christians don't do witnessing; they are witnesses—good or bad. Concentrate on improving your witness for Jesus Christ.

7. In your own words, re-write Romans 10:13-15.

_____

_____

_____

_____

Some people never read the Bible and seldom attend church. If you want them to know what Christ can do for them, let them see what Christ has done for you.

8. Peter wrote some encouraging instructions regarding witnessing to Christians who were enduring significant suffering. They are still applicable today.

a. What suggestions does Peter make regarding witnessing in 1 Peter 3:15-16?

_____

_____

_____

b. Which of these do you think is the most important and why?

_____

_____

9. What are some steps you could take to become a more effective witness?

_____

_____

_____

> *You are writing a Gospel, a chapter each day,*
> *by the deeds that you do and the words that you say.*
> *Men read what you write—distorted or true;*
> *What is the Gospel according to you?*

SUMMARY

God has summoned each Christian to be a witness of what he has "seen and heard" (1 John 1:3). Witnessing is a style of living—you are a witness at all times. You witness by your life. Actions are often more revealing than words. Your actions, however, are not sufficient to communicate to another the message of the Gospel of Christ. You also need to witness by your words—to identify openly with Jesus Christ and speak to others the message of how man can be reconciled to God. One very effective means of communicating to another person is the story of how God has worked in your life.

Keep Growing . . .

WHAT YOU HAVE ACCOMPLISHED

During *Growing Strong in God's Family* you have taken significant steps toward firmly establishing your walk with Christ. Your Christian life has been built up by:

- Learning to enjoy Bible reading.
- Experiencing a consistent and meaningful quiet time with the Lord, and recording daily quiet time thoughts.
- Memorizing five key Scripture passages for developing your walk with Christ, and deepening your convictions about the importance of memorizing Scripture.
- Discovering in Bible study the principles of maintaining a balanced Christian life.
- Developing an Evangelism Prayer List and considering ways to develop contact with non-Christians.

Congratulations on your diligence in completing *Growing Strong in God's Family*!

THE 2:7 SERIES

> *"Rooted and built up in him, strengthened in the faith as you were taught, and overflowing with thankfulness."* —Colossians 2:7

As you know, only those who have graduated from *Growing Strong in God's Family* may take Course 1 in *The 2:7 Series.*

What is the purpose of *The 2:7 Series?* What the Holy Spirit expresses through Paul in Colossians 2:7 clearly defines the specific goals of this training:

1. For a Christian to become *built up* in Christ and *established* in his faith. This series of courses includes instruction in practical Bible study techniques, Scripture memory skills, how to sharpen your devotional life, and how to be effective in evangelism. The objective is to become consistent in these disciplines rather than just accumulating Bible knowledge.
2. For a Christian to learn to *overflow with gratitude* in everyday life. The series will help an individual learn to experience and enjoy a stable and consistent Christian walk.
3. For a Christian to be *instructed.* This implies that training must take place before people develop into the kind of Christian laypeople who can impact their community.

What are some of the results of *The 2:7 Series?* Many who have been trained through this series have developed qualities enabling them to assume greater responsibilities and become more effective in their local churches. Marriages and families have been helped as individual members have grown spiritually and become firmly established in their walks with God. After graduating from this series of courses these maturing Christians have additional tools to help others in their growth in Christ and in reaching out to non-Christians.

Pray and carefully evaluate your situation before you begin *The 2:7 Series.* Each of *The 2:7 Series* courses lasts about three months. They require 1-3 hours of homework preparation each week and the class sessions are 1½-2 hours long. Ask the Lord to lead you. Get advice from your *Growing Strong in God's Family* leader. *The 2:7 Series* is excellent training. You will benefit greatly from it if you are able to schedule time to do the work thoroughly and on time.

Notes

PAGE	SOURCE
26	J. Oswald Sanders, *Pursuit of the Holy* (Grand Rapids: Zondervan, 1972).
33	John R.W. Stott, *Basic Christianity* (Downers Grove, Illinois: InterVarsity Press, 1958).
43	John R.W. Stott, *Understanding the Bible* (Glendale, California: Gospel Light Publications, 1972).
51	J. Oswald Sanders, *Spiritual Leadership* (Chicago: Moody Press, 1967).
55	Oswald Chambers, *My Utmost for His Highest* (New York: Dodd, Mead and Company, 1935).
64	John R.W. Stott, *Basic Christianity* (Downers Grove, Illinois: InterVarsity Press, 1958).
71	Paul Little, *How to Give Away Your Faith* (Downers Grove, Illinois: InterVarsity Press, 1966).

Notes

Leader's Guide

LEADER'S GUIDE
GROWING STRONG IN GOD'S FAMILY
OVERVIEW

SESSION #	1	2	3	4	5	6	7	8	9	10
SCRIPTURE MEMORY	Beginning with Christ Explanation; How to Memorize a Verse Effectively	1 John 5:11-12	How to Review Memory Verses Together; John 16:24	1 Corinthians 10:13		1 John 1:9	Proverbs 3:5-6	Review all 5 Beginning with Christ verses →		Why Memorize Scripture
QUIET TIME	How to Mark Your Bible as You Read; Where to Read in Your Bible; Reading and Marking Exercise		Share highlights from Bible reading →; How to Use My Personal Reading Record		How to Use Your Highlights Record; Why Use the Highlights Record; The Quiet Time; Quiet Time Reading Plans, and Bible Study	Share thoughts from Bible Reading Highlights Record →				
BIBLE STUDY		Introduction to Bible Study; Beginning with Christ Bible Study	"Christ the Center"	"Obedience"		"The Word"		"Prayer"	"Fellowship"	"Witness"
PRAYER				Practical Suggestions on Prayer		Evangelism Prayer List	Guide to Conversational Prayer			
OTHER	How Growing Strong in God's Family Came About; General Comments		Tyranny of the Urgent		Completion Record	Developing Contacts with Non-Christians			The Wheel Illustration	A Personal Evaluation of the Wheel in My Life; Keep Growing

Preface

The Title

The title, *Growing Strong in God's Family,* suggests the goal of this course and the context in which it will be used.

1. The goal is individual spiritual growth. The course is designed to strengthen participants in the basics of Christian life and ministry.
2. This course is designed and prepared for local church use—whether the discussion group is held in the church building or in a home.
3. After each lesson is prepared individually, it should be discussed in a group with others who have also prepared the lesson.

Important

1. Leader's Guide

   It is important for one person to act as the leader during each group meeting. This may be the same person each time or the responsibility may be shared by two or three group members.

   This leader's guide is based on extensive field testing of *Growing Strong in God's Family* and *The 2:7 Series.* It is imperative for the group leader to use this material each and every week as part of his or her careful preparation. The leader's guide is filled with proven principles, methods, and suggestions. Using it can significantly lighten the preparation load for a group leader.

2. Leader Training Clinics

   Excellent leader training clinics are available once or twice a year in many areas of the United States, Canada, and in several other countries. GROUP LEADERS WHO HAVE INVESTED A FEW HOURS IN A LEADER TRAINING CLINIC WILL BE ABLE TO MAXIMIZE THE EFFECTIVENESS OF *GROWING STRONG IN GOD'S FAMILY.* The leader training clinic is not mandatory before leading *Growing Strong in God's Family* but is strongly recommended!

   Information about training clinics may be obtained from Church Discipleship Ministries, The Navigators, P.O. Box 6000, Colorado Springs, CO 80934. The telephone number is (303) 598-1212.

Group Size

The professionals in the field of small group discussions say that 4-8 people make for the best discussions. For this course, PLAN ON 8-10 PARTICIPANTS IN YOUR GROUP—not including yourself. You may find it necessary to have more. Just remember that each person over 10 diminishes the impact of this course one more notch. It is wiser to break a group of 12 or more into two groups when possible. Your only limitation may be the number of qualified group leaders available.

Study Books

It is imperative that each person in your group have his or her own copy of *Growing Strong in God's Family*. People should write their name or put an address label on their book for easy identification.

Each person will be expected to do homework every week. It is motivational for an individual to complete his own work and fill in his own answers. By the end of the course, *Growing Strong in God's Family* will have become a valued possession and will be a personal reference book for many years to come. With this in mind, suggest that the members of your group make neat and legible entries as they go through the course.

Getting Started

The following guidelines should be of great value in helping you start a group in *Growing Strong in God's Family*. You will want to refer to them often as you continue through this course.

The Benefits of Being a Discipleship Group Leader

As a leader of a *Growing Strong in God's Family* group, you will see the cause of Christ advanced in these two ways:

1. Growth in the spiritual lives of others.
2. Growth in your own spiritual life.

This growth will come about not as a result of this leader's guide, but as you learn from your own experiences, as you apply the resources you have, and as you maintain high expectations.

This leader's guide is not the final authority on how to lead your group. Each leader and each group is unique. But the information included here can offer you significant help.

Remember that the *Growing Strong in God's Family* study is only a means to an end. These are excellent and proven materials. However, publications and programs do not make disciples. Only a disciple can make a disciple. It is imperative that you practice what you teach. Only as the spirit of God works in a life can there be significant and lasting changes. These concepts should guide your thinking as you help each member of your group grow toward spiritual maturity in Christ.

Your Goals as Group Leader

You have two long-range goals when helping people become functioning disciples:

1. To help each person become a more mature disciple of Jesus Christ.
2. To equip each person with the tools and know-how to help him or her make disciples of others.

Give each person in your group the opportunity to develop the qualities, habits, and discipline that mark him or her as a man or woman of God. They need to be growing in their relationships both with God and with other people.

Members of your group also need to be encouraged to share with others some of the things they are learning during the group sessions and what they are experiencing in their walk with God.

Evaluating Your Progress

Use the following questions (and your own) to evaluate your leadership.

Who?   Who am I serving?
        Who are the people in my group? Do I really know them?
What?   What are my goals for *Growing Strong in God's Family* and what are my goals for each session?
        What needs and expectations do my group members have?
Where? Where am I in my own Christian life?
        Where am I taking this group?
Why?   Why am I leading this group?
        Why is each person in my group?
When?   When will we reach our goals?
        When will I spend time socially with members of my group?
How?   How do we achieve our goals?

Getting Organized

1. Since you need at least an hour and a half for each session in the *Growing Strong in God's Family* study, the Sunday school hour is usually not long enough to serve as a meeting time. So when should you meet? Your final decision may involve some sacrifice on your part—you may have to give up a night or an afternoon each week that you wanted to save for yourself. But, after all, you've decided to serve this group, so find out what time is best for your group.

Consider such things as the types of jobs your group members have. For example, those with construction jobs or other outside work may prefer not to meet in the early evening. But people who commute to work early in the mornings may not want to be out late at night. Couples with young children may have days or times that are easiest for them to find babysitters. Assess your group's needs and encourage each member to be willing to compromise some if necessary.

2. Where will you meet—at church, in your home, in the homes of other group members, or somewhere else? You may find that a rotation system is best, in which you take turns going to each other's homes. This allows everyone to share the responsibility for hosting the group, and also divides the driving time.

Whatever you work out, try to find comfortable surroundings that encourage group involvement. You will have from eight to twelve people who need room to interact in a relaxed way. You want to sit in a circle so you can all see each other and talk easily with one another. There are times when the group divides briefly into twos and threes.

3. What about refreshments? Let the group decide how much effort, if any, they want to give to this. Preparing refreshments shouldn't become a burden to anyone. Be sure to keep them simple.

4. The presence of children during the meeting can be a distraction. What arrangements do your group members need to make for babysitting?

5. Should you allow for informal socializing before the scheduled meeting time, with the group arriving early for this? Or would they prefer to begin the session when they arrive, and use the time afterward for talking? Discuss this and set a policy that will help them plan when to come and how long to stay.

Handling Potential Problems

Your group may face a few of the problems listed here. By considering them in advance, you will be better able to deal with them should they occur.

- Frequent absences
- Frequent tardiness
- Lack of preparation
- Lack of motivation
- Difficulties in relating to each other or to you
- Members who drop out
- Varying degrees of expectations and interest
- Members who seem to monopolize the group's time
- Considerations that require changing your regular meeting time
- Couples in which the husband and wife seem to be going different directions in their interests and expectations
- Members who are experiencing "dry" periods in their spiritual lives

Difficulties such as these will not simply go away. You must handle them in an attitude of love and concern, so be prepared to do so. Here are several suggestions:

1. Talk alone with the persons involved. Share with them your concern and your desire for their success.

2. Establish a satisfactory agreement with the persons involved or with the group as a whole. This will make them accountable to each other.

3. Share some concerns with the entire group. Point out your goals as their leader and your desire for them to share these goals with you. Always do this in a positive, encouraging manner.

4. Give occasional "locker room chats"—in a gracious, loving way—to remind, encourage, and correct.

5. Feel free to talk seriously about relevant biblical principles that deal with problem areas.

6. Seek outside help from your pastor or from other mature Christians when necessary.

Getting Together

1. Start and end on time. Most people appreciate punctuality. Don't allow the time to get away from you at the end. You want the group to be anxious to return next week.

2. Try to involve each group member in all of the discussions.

3. Avoid embarrassing anyone. Some may feel uncomfortable at first in such activities as praying aloud or group discussions.

4. As the leader, participate in all the activities. A new group especially needs to see your example.

5. Be sure any instructions you give are clearly understood.

6. Be yourself. Use the outlines given in the leader's guide for each session, but don't be mechanical about it.

7. Be prepared. The others will be discouraged if you do not seem to know what you are doing, especially after they have taken the time themselves to prepare.

8. Have your goals clearly in mind for each session.

Between Meetings

Your commitment to the group includes more than just the giving of your time to the group session itself. Accomplishing your goal of making disciples will require additional activities on your part.

1. Are you establishing a caring relationship with each person? Get to know them apart from your time in the group. The stronger your relationship with each one outside the group, the more productive the group sessions will be.

2. Are you praying regularly for each group member?

3. How are you growing as a Christian? To succeed as a leader, you must keep growing yourself.

4. Remember your priorities. Don't let your responsibilities to the group override your personal relationship with God or your responsibilities to your family.

Guidelines for Growing Strong in God's Family

For many members of your group, this course will probably mean the beginning of consistent and meaningful quiet times, the beginning of Scripture memory, and the beginning of group Bible study—habits that should bring them into a closer relationship with Jesus Christ.

Goals for *Growing Strong in God's Family*

In this course you will want to help your group achieve these goals:

1. To enjoy reading the Bible.

2. To memorize the five *Beginning with Christ* verses.

3. To experience consistent and meaningful quiet times.

4. To complete *The Wheel Illustration* Bible study.

5. To study and discuss *Tyranny of the Urgent.*

6. To become familiar with *The Wheel Illustration.*

7. To make and use an Evangelism Prayer List.

A Flowchart for *Growing Strong in God's Family*
This flowchart shows how various aspects of the Christian life are emphasized in this course:

Bible Study

The Wheel Illustration—Sessions 3-10
"Quiet Time, Reading Plans, and Bible Study"—Session 5.

Prayer

Prayer is a regular ingredient in all ten sessions.
"Practical Suggestions on Prayer"—Session 4.
"Guide to Conversational Prayer"—Session 7.

Scripture Memory

"How to Memorize a Verse Effectively"—Session 1.
Memorizing the five *Beginning with Christ* verses—Sessions 2-7.
"*Beginning with Christ* Bible Study"—Session 2.
"How to Review Memory Verses Together"—Session 3.
"Why Memorize Scripture?"—Session 10.

Quiet Time

"How to Mark Your Bible as You Read"—Session 1.
"Where to Read in Your Bible"—Session 1.
"Reading and Marking Exercise"—Session 1.
"Quiet Time, Reading Plans, and Bible Study"—Session 5.
Sharing quiet time highlights—Sessions 2-10.
"How to Use Your *Bible Reading Highlights Record*"—Session 5.
"Why Use the *Bible Reading Highlights Record*"—Session 5.
"The Quiet Time"—Session 5.
"Quiet Time, Reading Plans, and Bible Study"—Session 5.

The Obedient Christian Life

Tyranny of the Urgent—Session 3.
The Wheel Illustration—Session 9.
"A Personal Evaluation of the Wheel in My Life"—Session 10.

Evangelism and Witness

"Why Have an Evangelism Prayer List"—Session 6.
"Setting Up Your Evangelism Prayer List"—Session 6.
"Developing Contacts with Non-Christians"—Session 6.

Preparing to Lead *Growing Strong in God's Family*

Don't neglect your own planning, even though the outlines in this guide for each group session are fairly detailed. Become familiar now with the overall thrust of the course, the goals toward which you are working, and the schedule for completing the specifics of the course.

Here are general reminders to pass on to your group:

1. Plan ahead to complete the required number of quiet times and the verse review assignments. It's a little late to get started when Session 9 rolls around.
2. Use a modern translation or paraphrase of the Scriptures for reading. Point out that this requirement is not for Bible study. It is for their daily reading and marking and will help make these times more fun and refreshing.
3. Use the *Bible Reading Highlights Record* and *My Personal Reading Record*. These will be new tools for most of the group.
4. Pray for each other and for the group as a whole.
5. Be sure to continually review the verses you have memorized.
6. Don't forget the starting time for the meetings.
7. In Session 5 immediately begin getting things signed off on the *Completion Record*. Don't let yourself get behind.

A group leader must be an example of a positive, Christ-centered lifestyle with consistent disciplines. Be sure you are regularly studying, memorizing, and meditating on the Scriptures. Spend regular time in prayer. Evaluate the balance in your Christian life by relating it to *The Wheel Illustration* in Session 9.

How to Make the Bible Study Discussions Effective

Group Leader Resource Material

It is important for you to carefully prepare so you can do a good job of leading each of the Bible study discussions. The following material has been compiled to assist you in handling the seven Bible study group discussions.

Usually each of the 10 sessions in *Growing Strong in God's Family* is led by the same group leader. Because of a group leader being sick, traveling, or some other contingency, it may be necessary for someone else from the group to take a turn leading one of the 10 sessions. The group leader for sessions 2, 3, 4, 6, 8, 9 and 10 will be leading a Bible study discussion as well as the other course activities. Each time you prepare to lead, you will want to refer to the suggestions in this section.

Student Preparation

A key ingredient to stimulating and beneficial Bible study discussions is for each member in the group to have his or her Bible study completed before coming to class.

From time to time remind the members of the group how important it is (for you and for them) to have the Bible study done prior to the group meeting. If someone comes without the study completed or partially finished, don't ignore or punish him with non-verbal looks of disapproval. Make him feel accepted and as much a part of the group as the others. It is important for that person to enjoy and benefit from the group discussion and not be made to feel rejected and unaccepted. At the beginning of the discussion you might assign that person one or two questions that can be quickly prepared and ready for discussion when you get to that part of the lesson.

Group Leader Preparation

First, prepare the Bible study for your own enlightenment and application. Ask God to speak to you and to strengthen you from the study as you begin to work on it. You want correct and good answers without being academic and theoretical. If you get excited about the topic of the study and its content, you are well on your way to being an exciting and animated group leader.

Second, look over your questions and answers. Think of the needs and interests in your group. To which parts of the study should you give more attention? Thinking through and planning in advance can make for a more effective Bible study discussion. During the actual Bible discussion you may find it wise to deviate from your original plan. Thoughtful preplanning gives you a general direction in which to move, but you must remain flexible and willing to adjust your original plan.

The Bible Says . . .

In your group you want people sharing what the Bible teaches, not opinions and conjectures. On one hand we don't want people to be afraid of making theological mistakes. On the other hand we don't want people sharing opinions and hearsay without a passage or two of Scripture to back up their comments. Mostly, this problem can be alleviated by sticking with the verses, questions, and answers in the Bible study. Don't let the discussion drift into tangents where you and the group members have not done your homework. Stick with the subject at hand.

Several Helpful Discussion Guidelines

1. Sit in a circle. This is the best seating arrangement. Each person has eye contact with most of the people in the group. It creates an informal and warm atmosphere. The group leader is considered more of a peer because he or she is not placed in a dominant physical location.
2. Don't dominate. As the leader, you are both a facilitator and a participant in the group. You should not talk more than others in the group. As the facilitator you give direction and ask questions. As a participant you share your insights and study answers along with the others. Share humbly, not as an expert.
3. Not the authority. Avoid becoming the authority figure in the group. You don't want all the questions directed to you with the others thinking that you should be able to answer them. Direct questions back to the group. Say something like, "That is an interesting question.

What thoughts might some of you have that would help us answer that question?" Sometimes you might recruit a volunteer who will take a difficult question to the pastor or an associate pastor. The volunteer can come back to the group with an answer the following week.

4. Work together. Your role as group leader is not a teaching responsibility just as the students' role is not to sit, listen and take notes. You and the group members are working together to find answers and clarify issues.

5. Too talkative. You will soon find the one or two people in your group who have something to say about everything. Chat with them on the side. Say something like, "You have some great ideas. You are excellent in the discussion times. I need your help. There are others in the group who need to talk more so they can grow in confidence. Could you help me in getting some of these people to talk more? Before you talk in the group, let one or two others go first. Don't be afraid of silence. It sometimes takes some silence before (name) and (name) will talk. Maybe you could share only your best thoughts in the group. Thank you for your help in this!"

6. Too quiet. When you direct a question to the group, give the quiet people more eye contact. Sometimes ask one of your less vocal people to read a quotation or to answer a specific question.

   A number of things in the general structure of *Growing Strong in God's Family* are designed to build confidence and help people participate more comfortably. Reading around the circle helps bring people out of their shells. Quoting verses and working on the *Completion Record* in groups of two or three each week also nurtures a growing confidence and security.

7. Acknowledge answers. Thank people when they participate. Thank them for reading a paragraph or answering a question. This is particularly important with those who tend to be quiet. An acknowledgement doesn't always have to be verbal. Many times it can be a nod of the head or eye contact that communicates approval. As you apply this, others in the group will follow your example and begin doing it.

8. Ask the group. Usually you will address your questions to the group, not to an individual. (An exception to this would be to ask a quiet person a specific question). As you ask a question, let your eye contact sweep around the group. Don't let your eyes lock in on one person.

9. Get several answers. After one person has given an answer to a Bible study question, you will usually ask for two more people to give their answers to the same question. This allows several people to participate on each question. It also helps insure that the answers reflect a correct handling of that particular Scripture passage.

   A simple question should be answered by only one or two people. A more difficult question could be answered by three or four people. Thought and application questions could be answered by half of the group or more if you wish.

   Have people read their answers exactly the way they have written them down. This keeps things moving. After they have read their written answers they might wish to express an ad lib sentence or two for clarification.

10. Application questions. In the *Growing Strong in God's Family* Bible studies you will find a
    sprinkling of application questions. These questions encourage us to use and apply the
    truths taught in the lesson. Be careful not to rush over the answers to these questions.
    Application questions need to be given a high priority. Some application questions may be
    so important that you will ask all the people in your group to share their answers.

    Here are some examples of application questions:
    1. Page 27, questions 8a and 8b.
    2. Page 45, 2nd part of question 10.
    3. Page 54, question 8c.
    4. Page 55, questions 9c and 9d.
    5. Page 73, question 9.

The "Think About" Questions

You may have observed that there is a "Think About" question at the beginning of each of the last
six Bible studies. Remind the group members to give two or three minutes of thought to the "Think
About" question before starting to prepare their Bible study. Its purpose is to get the mind moving
in the direction that the Bible study topic will be going.

You will notice that there are no correct or "school" answers to "Think About" questions.
They are designed to stimulate thinking and precipitate a wide range of answers.

How to Lead the Bible Study Discussion

In the seven Bible studies, your goal will be to have every question answered by at least one person.
When an answer is simple and straightforward, you can usually move right on to the next question.
When an answer is more complex, generates a variety of answers, or hits an area of special interest,
you will need to invest more time and welcome the answers and comments from more people.

During this course group leaders will want to use both of the following methods in leading
the discussion.

1. Question-by-question—sharing in sequence. Go around the circle in turn and have each
   person answer one question or sub-question. Go through the questions in order. (See "8.
   Ask the group" and "9. Get several answers" on page 87). It is recommended that you use
   this method at least through Session 4. Often people like this approach because of its
   predictability.

   As you go around the circle, also have people read aloud the quotations and
   paragraphs between questions.

   When you start the discussion, tell the group where you want them to begin in the
   circle and whether you want them to go to the left or to the right. Don't always start in the
   same place or go in the same direction. Share your answer or read a quotation when it is
   your turn.

2. Question-by-question—sharing at random. In this method *do not* go around the circle in
   sequence, but still answer the Bible study questions in order. Work on a volunteer basis.

You might ask, "Would someone please read the opening paragraph?" Someone says, "I will," and reads it. After it has been read, ask, "Who will answer question 1 for us please?"

Continue on with question 2, then question 3. Have the quotations and paragraphs read in between questions as you did in the previous method.

Occasionally quieter students in the group may need to be asked something like, "John, would you answer question 6 for us please?" Then go back to the volunteer approach again. (Still apply "Ask the group" and "Get several answers" on page 87).

It is not recommended to use this method before Session 5.

In the leader's guide for Sessions 6, 8, 9, and 10 you are given some additional Bible study discussion questions. If you have attended a leader training clinic or have been in *The 2:7 Series*, you know how and when to use them effectively. To begin with, use them sparingly. If your group responds to them, you may wish to use them more in Sessions 9 and 10.

You may not yet have attended a leader training clinic or been in *The 2:7 Series*. It is still very effective to lead the discussions by using only the two methods explained above. Here is a brief explanation if you wish to try out a few of the additional questions.

One of these additional questions should only be asked after the designated question has been answered. Look at question 4 on page 52. An answer to the John 15:7 question will have the word "abide" (or equivalent) in it. When someone shares an answer to the John 15:7 question, you might ask, "What do you think the word 'abide' means?" This type of question often stimulates further and deeper discussion. After discussing the meaning of the word "abide," continue where you left off in the lesson.

Additional help for leading Bible study discussions is available at *The 2:7 Series* leader training clinics, and from the NavPress book, *How to Lead Small Group Bible Studies*.

Session 1

1. Get acquainted.
Have each member of the group answer these questions:

    a. What is your name?

    b. What is your job?

    c. Where did you grow up?

It is important that the leader be the first to answer those questions. This gives the students an idea of how much time to take. You might say something like: "We are going to spend a few minutes getting acquainted. Some of you know each other quite well, but this will give me an opportunity to get acquainted with you. I think that what we're going to do now will be interesting and fun. I would like each of you as we go around the circle to tell us your name, your job, and where you grew up. Why don't I start and then we can go around the circle to the left (or right)."

The primary goal is to break the ice and to get to know each other. Some people have never shared Scripture truths, or prayed, in a group. Therefore, another goal is to make people comfortable about talking in the group. Each group member should participate in this first session.

2a. Read how *Growing Strong in God's Family* Came About" (page 7).
Have it read aloud by one person or by several. After it has been read, you may wish to give a brief testimony of the significance of *Growing Strong in God's Family* in your own life or in the lives of others you know. Keep it brief and vital.

2b. Read "General Comments" (page 8).
At this point we do *not* discuss the *Completion Record* or the details of the course. Covering these pages prematurely could be discouraging. For now, pages 7 and 8 are enough information for most students. You will fully explain the *Completion Record* in Session 5. By then they will have already completed about 1/3 of the requirements and will be motivated by their progress. Don't be secretive. Tell them what they want to know. But don't tell them more than they need to know at this point. Do answer any specific questions they ask.

3. Discuss how to make Bible reading exciting.
a. Use a contemporary translation or paraphrase.
This portion of the training session is a *short* lecture. The lecture might go something like this: "As other laypeople, pastors, and Christian workers have gone through this course they have found that two things make Bible reading exciting. The first is to use a contemporary translation or paraphrase."

"For Bible study you may have already selected a translation of the Bible which you feel best suits you and which is accepted by your church and associates. When we do Bible reading, however, we will often make it a practice to read one translation and then eventually to read several translations or paraphrases. This creates a freshness and excitement in our Bible reading which does not lose its sparkle over the months and years."

"So the first proven principle in making Bible reading exciting is for us to read from a contemporary translation or paraphrase. We do not recommend the *King James Version* for Bible reading in this course, though you will be able to use it for Bible study if you wish. For our next class session, you will need to have an inexpensive contemporary translation or paraphrase to use during the course."

You may need to explain some of the translations and paraphrases available and their distinctives. You might even bring samples to class for them to see.

Then continue with something like: "The second thing that will make Bible reading exciting is marking our Bibles as we read them. This enables us to make decisions as to what really impressed us. It will keep our reading from 'slipping through our fingers' without having really gleaned something." This will make a natural transition into the discussion of pages 8-9, "How to Mark Your Bible as You Read."

b. Study "How to Mark Your Bible as You Read" (pages 8-9).

Have two people read: one person reading through the six subpoints, and another person reading down to Isaiah 11:1-7. As the person completes reading the six subpoints, point out examples of the markings in the Scripture texts.

1. *Brackets* can be put around a phrase or even a sentence or two.
2. The short *diagonal lead-in line* refers to the phrase that immediately follows it.
3. The *parallel diagonal lines* in the margin should be used when the passage being marked is greater than one verse or is a very long verse.
4. The *circle* can be used for repeated words within a passage or to indicate the people who are the principals in that particular passage. Quite often a circle is used to mark some additional impression when reviewing a passage already marked in some other way.
5. A *vertical line in the margin* refers to the phrase or sentence(s) beside it.
6. *Underlining* can be used for phrases, repeated words, or a sentence. It is not good for whole sections. Too much underlining is tedious and meaningless.

The important point is to use various markings to highlight how the passage has impressed you. So caution the group not to get hung up on the "correct" technical use of a type of mark. They may even want to create markings of their own.

There are some people who, because of their backgrounds, have hesitated to mark in their Bibles. Some individuals dislike putting any marks in a book. Empathize with a student who feels this way, but encourage him to mark in his Bible in the same way the other students do. That is why a person needs to buy an inexpensive version of the Bible. The reading and marking aspect of the course is as necessary for graduating as is the memorizing of the five verses. Be understanding.

c. Study "Where to Read in Your Bible" (page 9).

The reason for not reading the Gospels consecutively is that the presentation is so similar (with the possible exception of John) that the students will tend to be impressed with some of the same things which they have just read in another Gospel. Thus, in order to have an effect on their personal lives, it will be more helpful to have them read one Gospel now and read another in a month or two. Also, the variety will keep their Bible reading fresh and interesting.

We want people to avoid the "grasshopper method" of Bible reading—that is the practice of jumping from place to place in the Bible. We want them to read one Bible book in sequence and complete it before starting another Bible book.

The usual pattern for reading and marking is to read one Bible book from beginning to end before going on to another old or new testament book.

Psalms and Proverbs are almost always interesting and practical in their content. Sometimes a person will get into a book that seems to be dry or heavy reading. You can suggest that the book be read concurrently with Psalms or Proverbs. You might recommend that students save Psalms and Proverbs for just such occasions and not read them all the way through at one time. This is one important exception to our rule about completing one book before going on to another.

There are two methods for reading two books concurrently. One method is to read a chapter out of each every day. The other method is to read out of one book one day and the other book on the next day. Students enjoy both of these methods, so it is really up to the individual to choose which method he would like to use. (The students should be advised not to read in more than two books of the Bible at one time. It is too difficult to maintain adequate continuity.)

4. Complete the "Reading and Marking Exercise" (pages 9-10).

Explain that they are going to read and mark Romans 12 using what they have just learned on pages 8-9. Explain that they will have 5-7 minutes to meditate on this passage, marking that which impresses them. They will be sharing what they have marked in a few minutes. Give them time to do the exercise and then share the results. Use this exercise both as an instructional tool and as an opportunity for interaction.

First share what you marked. Don't "steal the best stuff." Share one or two small things. You have done much of the talking so far in this class. Now encourage each group member to talk. Expect each person to say something. Thank each one as he or she finishes sharing.

5. Introduce the *Beginning with Christ* memory material (pages 10-13).

Before showing the students how to effectively memorize Scripture, show them what memory work they will be expected to complete during this course. You might say something like: "During this course one of the most exciting things that you will be doing is memorizing five key Bible passages. If you never memorized another verse, these five would be the most helpful verses you could memorize! Right now you need to decide in what version you are going to memorize them."

Have them turn to the verse cards in the back of the book and explain the alternatives. Give them whatever help they need in making this decision. Explain that they will be studying "*Beginning with Christ* Explanation" for the next session. They will be filling out pages 15-17 based on what they find as they study the material.

6. Read "How to Memorize a Verse Effectively" (page 13).

Once again have the students do the reading. This continues to help them become comfortable speaking in the group. As the leader, it is important that you have experienced everything taught in these pages and have proven the principles to be effective through your own experience. You can even do some of these things just a few days ahead of the group.

As they go through page 13, it is important that the students understand the principles set forth. The objective is not so much to force the student to do these things as it is for him to understand the principles on this page. If a student has trouble with the Scripture memory work, it will be because one or more of these principles are being neglected.

Students may memorize any way they wish. You are not forcing them to do it a certain way. They just need to understand that in order to graduate from this course they will have to say the five passages of Scripture without any mistakes.

Remind your group to use the following principles for effective memorization. Remember, thousands of people have proven the value of these principles during the last 50 years.

1. *Preliminary work.*

It is important for a student to do some minimal preliminary work before actually starting to memorize the verse(s) on a memory card. The card should be read aloud a few times. The meaning needs to be understood. You or someone else in the group may need to explain a verse or part of a verse.

2. *Topic, reference and first phrase.*

The student should not just skim over the topic and reference to get into the actual content of the verse. The topic and reference are just as important as the content of the verse. If one has the topics clearly in mind, he will be able to use the verses he memorizes with greater skill. If the student knows a reference, he is able to turn to the passage and use it.

It is very important to immediately connect the last part of the reference with the first part of the verse. There should be no pause between stating the reference and starting the verse. If the student must pause to recall how the verse begins, he should then start over and say the topic, reference, and immediately start into the verse itself. This insures that the topic and reference are inseparably tied to the verse.

3. *Add phrases.*

If the student continues to add phrases to what has been memorized, he should never have a problem with transposing the contents of the verse. The shorter amount of time a student spends memorizing a given verse, the more important it is for him to review that verse to keep from losing his ability to quote it exactly.

4. *Audibly.*

If the student can speak audibly in a normal conversational tone, it will aid his success in memory work. This may be no more than whispering or simply moving his lips when working on a verse. Saying the verse aloud as it is being memorized makes us use more of our senses and makes a deeper impression on the mind.

5. *Apply the verse to your life.*

The more impact a verse has when applied to the student's life, the easier it is to memorize and retain it. Think about what this verse means "to me."

6. *Sequence.*

If a student ignores the sequence in which the topic, reference, and verse are quoted, he will often find himself in trouble later in recalling all three important parts of the memorized verses. In using a verse with someone else, he may not audibly say the topic and reference, but the topic and reference should go through his mind before he quotes the verse audibly. When he says only the verse without the topic and reference, he has given the verse some of his review time, but he has neglected to review the other two integral parts of his memory work. All three parts must be reviewed every time if the student is to be successful at Scripture memory.

It is important to always say the reference after quoting the verse. After committing a number of verses to memory and perhaps neglecting the review of a few verses, the student may only recall the last part of the verse and be unable to say the first part. If the reference is an integral part of the end of the verse as well as the beginning, he can then pick up the location of that verse from only knowing the last part of the verse.

7a. *Review, Review, Review!*

Call someone by name and have him read paragraph 7a. This is a very crucial part of our Scripture memory work.

7b. The principle of overlearning is an essential concept. Many people make the mistake of thinking they really know a memory verse when they are able to say the verse without any help. We know that this is not really true.

Psychologists use the term "overlearning" for the process of learning something so well that we can recall it with little or no hesitation. We have overlearned our name, our telephone number, our address, the names of friends, and routes we travel in our car. It is not until we have gone through the process of overlearning that we really know a verse. Then, the Spirit of God can bring it to mind whenever He would choose to use it. The key to overlearning is repetition.

7. Read the "Assignment for Session 2" (page 13).

Have one person read the assignment.

8. Pray.

Lead in a closing prayer.

Session 2

1. Get further acquainted.

This is the last session in which a new student may join the group. Therefore, it is important to have some type of activity for getting acquainted in this session.

Even though all of the students at the first session went through a get-acquainted exercise, it is still helpful to break the ice again so the students feel increasingly comfortable in the group. Go around the circle and have each student answer these questions:

    a. What is your name?

    b. What is your favorite breakfast?

    c. What is your favorite hobby?

2. Review Session 1.

Comment on some of the highlights up through page 13. For example, on page 8, "General Comments", simply say there are 10 sessions in this course; there will be requirements which must be met in order to graduate; most weeks they will spend an hour in preparation. Review the rest of the material in a similar manner. It will be important, however, for you or a member of the group to meet with anyone who missed Session 1 and review the material in greater detail.

3. Share with the group what you read and marked in your Bible this week.

The major portion of Session 2 will be sharing. It is important that the students learn to share what they have been reading in the Scriptures. In fact, the sharing time becomes a highlight for most and a breakthrough for many who have never shared in a group before.

It is important for you as the leader to remember the following: (1) nothing is too simple to be shared; (2) the students should feel free to share more than once; (3) it should be an unhurried time; (4) those who haven't read will find the group pressure strong during the sharing time, and they will be motivated to read the following week; and (5) it may be necessary to remind the students that they are not competing with each other.

It is important for you as the leader to share first, so the rest of the students will know what you expect from them. Every time you share from your reading share something (1) SIMPLE and (2) ENCOURAGING! Then ask group members to share spontaneously, rather than going around the circle.

You will want to communicate to them that normally everyone is expected to share something every week.

4. Break into groups of two or three and review 1 John 5:11-12.

At this point have the group break up into small groups of two or three, made up of persons who are memorizing from the same version. At this time husbands and wives should *not* review together. Tell the students that as they quote the verse assigned for this week they must be sure to say the topic, reference, verse, and reference. You should allow 5-10 minutes for review together each week.

Group members may want to scatter throughout the room where you meet, or even into other rooms where there are fewer distractions. As the leader, you will not want to try to control everything in the session. Let your students take the initiative. They can easily figure out what to do if you give them some idea of what you expect.

5. Review memory methods.

This is a brief lecture in which you emphasize three main points:

a. Practice aloud.

This allows another one of the senses—hearing—to be involved in the memory process. This helps memorization greatly. The student will want to practice aloud whenever possible. You may wish to ask if any of the students found this helpful during the last week. Do not reprimand those who have not done it, but commend those who have tried it.

b. Spot and correct repeated errors.

An example of a repeated error would be leaving out an "and" or adding the word "and" in 1 John 5:11-12. Another example would be using the wrong beginning word. It is important to communicate to the students that this is a natural part of the process of learning a verse. It does not mean that they have failed in their memory work. When they get to the point where there might be one or two repeated errors within a verse, they can easily correct these errors after they have been identified and isolated.

c. Review is the key.

You must be setting the example for your students in this! Sharing personal benefits and brief testimonials from time to time will continue to motivate them. The three principles in any kind of memorization are:

    Repetition
    Impression
    Association

Repetition is the primary memory principle that applies to Scripture memory. The slogan is "Review, review, review!" Constant review can insure long and meaningful retention.

Impression is concentrating intently so that something makes a deeper imprint on your mind, concentrating intently as a person tells you his name, for example. Focusing your mental effort produces a more lasting impression of what you hear or see.

Association is a technique where you use some gimmick to aid your recall. You may remember that the Old Testament contains 39 books, that 3x9 is 27, and that there are 27 books in the New Testament. The 3x9 association aids recall.

6. Read "Introduction to Bible Study" (pages 14-15), and look over the first study, "Christ the Center" (pages 24-28).

7. Discuss the "*Beginning with Christ* Bible Study" (pages 15-17).

Ask for volunteers to answer each of the questions, or simply go around the circle and have one person take each of the questions. The subpoints of question 1 can be handled as individual questions if you like.

    The goal of the first seven questions is to ensure that each student has read and understands the written material in "*Beginning with Christ* Explanation" on pages 10-13.

    On question 5, have two or three people in your group give their answers.

    You should also have more than one person answer questions 8, 10, 12, 14 and 16. These questions lead to more individual analysis and the answers tend to stimulate good discussion.

8. Read the "Assignment for Session 3" (page 18).

Have someone read the assignment for Session 3.

9. Pray.

Ask someone in the group to close the session in prayer.

Session 3

1. Study "How to Review Memory Verses Together" (pages 19-20).

Have this section read aloud by the group members. Go around the circle and have each person take just one point or a sub-point.

The suggestion of reviewing the verses they know best first is an extension of the philosophy of constantly building upon successes rather than patching up failures. This approach gives the students an extra boost.

In this session you will work at developing a certain attitude, philosophy, or outlook among the students. The students should be trying to help each other succeed rather than competing with each other in order to excel. An excellent biblical illustration is found in Ecclesiastes 4:9-10, quoted on page 19.

Often a person will ask why it is so important to memorize verses exactly and to be so meticulous in memory work. Page 19 gives them four excellent reasons based on the experience of many people.

It is important to apply points 4 and 5 in each session. If the person listening to a verse being quoted gives the person quoting the verse more hints than he really desires, the listener is doing the quoter an injustice. If the one quoting the verse struggles and strains and finally comes up with the exact words of the verse, it will be a tremendous victory and a great encouragement to him.

Whether or not the listener had to help the quoter, it is helpful if the one doing the quoting repeats the verse again word perfectly after he has struggled with the verse. He will now realize how the verse should be quoted. This will end the Scripture memory time on a note of victory and accomplishment.

2. Break into groups of two or three and review 1 John 5:11-12 and John 16:24.

You will find that the previous discussion about Scripture memory will launch the students into their verse review with greater motivation. It will give them an immediate opportunity to apply the "listener" and "quoter" principles they have just learned.

Again, it is best for people to review their memory verses with someone else who is memorizing in the same version. *It is important that the listener always be looking at a verse card* as the quoter goes through a verse. This is true no matter how well the listener thinks he knows the verse being quoted.

After returning to the circle, you may ask: "How many of you were able to say at least one of the two verses without any mistakes at all?" Then you might commend them by saying: "That's really terrific; you are doing a fine job and that's great." You may then ask if any of them were able to say both verses without a mistake. Commend those people, too.

3. Share with the rest of the group what you read and marked in your Bible this week.

Prior to beginning the sharing of thoughts from their Bible reading, ask everyone to spend a minute or two deciding at least one thing they wish to share with the group.

It is not important for you to always share first. However, you may wish to share something first if no one else shares right away. Your example will stimulate the others to share.

This period of time should not be rushed. There is enough time for each person to share at least once from his reading. While you don't want those who share to go off into a long discourse, they can briefly develop what a particular verse or passage meant to them. Once again the students should be praised and thanked each time they share with the group. This can be something simple like: "That's a wonderful thought!" "That's a very interesting thought!" "Thank you for sharing that with us!" or "You certainly enjoyed reading that particular passage, didn't you?"

4. Discuss the article *Tyranny of the Urgent* (pages 20-24).

Remind them that during the discussion they may wish to take a few notes under item 4 on page 23. Have someone read the title and two quotations at the top. Have two or three share their answers to 1. Then have two or three share their answers to 2. Probably each person will want to share something on 3; some may share more than once. Don't go around the circle. Just have them share at random as they are ready to say something.

This is an outstanding article, but you will find that it does not take long to discuss it. The article is clearly written, and its message is simple to understand—though challenging to apply.

Take a few minutes to discuss as a group how *Tyranny of the Urgent* applies to taking this course. Ask several to share how they answered question 5 on page 24.

5. Discuss the Bible Study "Christ the Center" (pages 24-28).

As the group leader, you will be leading a Bible study 7 of the 10 weeks. (There is no Bible study scheduled for 3 of the 10 weeks). You will prepare your own Bible study just like every other member of the group. Then, in addition to your personal preparation you will need to prepare to lead. In this leader's guide you have been given helps to make preparation and leading easier for you. Be sure to carefully review "How to Make Bible Study Discussions Effective," pages 85-89 in this leader's guide. Apply the principles in preparing and leading this Bible study. The principles on pages 85-89 are designed to assist you whether you are a nervous beginner or a confident and experienced leader of small groups. PRAY. PREPARE. PARTICIPATE.

Start the "Christ the Center" Bible study discussion by having someone read the opening statement and paragraph.

Then, ask the group what some of their ideas and insights are from the "Think About" question: "What are some indicators of what is central in our lives?" Allow time for several to respond.

Have someone read question 1 on page 24. Then, let one person answer each of the four subpoints under question 1. Apply the principles under "Get several answers", page 87, in your leader's guide. Continue on through the Bible study discussion as you wish to lead it.

6. Go over "How to Use *My Personal Reading Record*" (pages 28-29).

Say something like: "Would each of you please turn to Romans on *My Personal Reading Record*. As you know, Romans is in the New Testament. You will notice that there are 16 numbers in little squares after the book of Romans. There are 16 chapters in Romans and each of these squares represents one of the chapters. So let's say that you or I spend some time today reading the first two chapters of Romans. After we have completed our reading, we will then put a diagonal line, or an "X", in boxes 1 and 2 after the title "Romans." This enables us to keep track of where we are reading, and it is encouraging to see the progress we are making.

7. Read the "Assignment for Session 4".
Have a student read the assignment on page 29.

8. Pray.
Have a student lead in prayer to close the session.

Session 4

---

1. Break into groups of two or three and review 1 John 5:11-12, John 16:24, and 1 Corinthians 10:13.
By now the students need very little guidance in doing their verse review. In this session simply say: "At this point, let's break into our verse review groups and go over the first three verses we've memorized."

2. Share with the rest of the group what you read and marked in your Bible this week.
Share your excitement about your Bible reading. If you are not excited, you can't expect your students to be excited. Often leaders cannot share the things that were most outstanding in their reading because they may be too advanced for the students. It is, therefore, important to look over your reading and select one or two items which are simple and encouraging and have them ready to share.

   As the leader, you may occasionally go first in the sharing just to get the ball rolling. Often, however, the students will be quite eager to share and will take the initiative. Remember to give them one or two minutes to refresh their memory and to prepare to share. Be alert to any who are not sharing from their reading. Draw them out. Before or after class find out if there are any problems.

3. Complete and discuss "Practical Suggestions on Prayer" (pages 30-33).
This is an exciting session—one you can look forward to and do with enthusiasm. Up to this point, the student has simply been reading the Scriptures. In a way, he has been having half a quiet time. Though you have never used the term "quiet time," the course attempts to help the student learn how to have a successful quiet time. In this session you will add the other half of a quiet time—prayer.

   1a. Ask two individuals to read 1 Corinthians 1:9 and 1 John 1:3. These are two excellent verses on the importance of fellowship with God. Spend just a few minutes discussing these verses and having everyone write a brief summary in the space provided on page 30.

   1b. After these two verses have been read, ask the question: "What are some of the ingredients which help us to have fellowship on a human level between two people? Perhaps if we can answer that, it will give us some clues as to how to better fellowship with God. What would you say are some of the ingredients in good fellowship with other people?"

Then let the students make as many comments as possible. They may say such things as honesty, love, mutual trust, time to talk together, and the need to discuss faults and failures as well as successes. Acknowledge whatever the students contribute and thank each student for his contribution. Commend the students for their participation, thank them, and show genuine appreciation for what they are saying. At this point in the course, actively sharing with each other is more important than the information they share.

1c. Give each student time to complete 1c. Then give several in the group a chance to share the two ingredients they selected as "very important."

1d. First, say something like this: "We have each chosen two ingredients that we feel are very important to fellowship with God. If we were to brainstorm together for a few minutes we might decide on four or five ingredients that we feel are the *more* important ones. But, there are two that we must have!"

"Under 1d, write in the two words 'listen' and 'talk'." (You might need to repeat this once or twice more.) "So, the fewest elements we can have and still have fellowship with someone are "They talk to me as I LISTEN and I TALK to them as they listen."

At this point you may say something like: "So in having true fellowship with God, He speaks to us as we are reading in the Scriptures; these are His words for us. Then as we pray to God and respond to Him through prayer, this completes the fellowship. If one person does all the talking and the other all the listening, that is not true fellowship. That is a lecture. If we do all the talking in prayer, and God does all the listening, that is not true fellowship. Nor is it fellowship if God does all the talking and we only listen."

Occasionally a student will suggest that God speaks to him in prayer as well as from the Scriptures. Ordinarily you would reply something like this: "Thank you for your comment. That is a good point. It is true that God impresses us occasionally with a certain thought while we are praying. Perhaps we could say that the *primary* way God speaks to us is through the Scriptures. The ability to sense that God is speaking to us about something, for example, while we are praying, is something that comes with spiritual maturity and is a result of obedience to God."

"In helping a new Christian establish fellowship with God, we will put the emphasis on spending consistent time in the Scriptures. The Scriptures reveal God's mind, and it is important for the young Christian to have God speak to him in this way. And, of course, we never outgrow the need to have God speak to us through the Scriptures. So we could say that God's primary and most consistent means of speaking with men and women is through his Word."

2. In the diagram, have everyone write "Word" in the left blank and "Pray" in the right blank. Then, have someone read aloud the sentence above the diagram and the paragraph below it.

As you know, "Word" is a synonym for the Bible. Some passages in the Scriptures use "the Word" to refer to Jesus Christ and others refer to the Bible. In the diagram, "Word" means the Bible.

3. In the diagram, have everyone write "Word" in the left blank, "Respond" on the top right, and "Other Prayer" at the bottom right. Have someone read aloud the paragraph above the diagram. Have someone else read aloud the rest of number 3 below the diagram.

One of the great benefits of "responding back to God in prayer" is that it makes the Word of God come alive in a new way! As a result, our fellowship with the Lord becomes more meaningful. We are meeting a Person, not a habit!

Encourage the members of your group to be practicing this method in their daily reading. Ask them to use the "effective communication" method during the coming week and be ready to share at the next session how it worked out for them.

4. Give the group 3 or 4 minutes to write in their comments under each of the two Scripture passages. Then ask two or three to share briefly what they wrote under the first one. Do the same with the second passage. Remember, we still have to discuss the Bible study on "Obedience." Keep things moving right along but don't rush them.

5. Have someone read the first two sentences. You may have the group work together on this question or have each person complete it individually.

If you plan to work together, get volunteers who will each read one of the seven passages. Have someone read the statement for 5a. Then, have the three verses read for 5a. Following the same pattern for 5b and 5c. The last person could also read the Spurgeon quotation—or have someone else read it. Once this is done, they can each check the boxes.

If you want them to complete this question individually, give them 4 or 5 minutes to look up each verse and check the boxes as they complete the work.

4. Discuss the Bible study "Obedience" (pages 33-36).

Each week continue to refer back to "How to Make the Bible Study Discussions Effective" on pages 85-89 in this leader's guide.

It is also very important to keep reviewing pages 80-85 in the leader's guide!

Have someone read the opening statement and quotation.

Read the "Think About" question aloud: "What are some similarities between the way children obey their parents and the way Christians obey God?" Ask how some in the group would answer it. Thank each participant. Remember that there is no "right" answer to a "Think About" question.

Have one person read the title, paragraph and question 1 below the "Think About" box. The same person should answer question 1. Apply the principles in "Get several answers", page 87, in this leader's guide.

Continue through the Bible study discussion "Obedience."

5. Read the "Assignment for Session 5" (page 36).

Ask someone to read this assignment. Then ask if there are any questions or comments about the assignment.

6. Pray.

Have someone close the session in prayer.

Session 5

1. Break into groups of two or three and review 1 John 5:11-12, John 16:24, and 1 Corinthians 10:13.

Have the students break up into verse review groups (as usual) and quote the three verses. After their review work, you might ask who was able to say all three verses word perfectly. Be sure to commend them for their good work.

Then express your excitement about this session. You might say something like: "This session is going to be one of the most helpful and exciting times we will have during this course, and I believe you will find it interesting. Let's share from what we've been reading and then we will get into some of the new material which I think you will find helpful and interesting."

2. Share with the group what you read and marked in your Bible this week.

You might open with a statement something like: "What are some of the interesting things you've been reading this week that you'd like to share with the rest of us? Are you finding that your reading and marking is becoming a meaningful practice?" Let the students respond. You don't want this to drag on and on, but you do want an indication of how the students are doing. Other questions you might ask are: "What books have you found particularly interesting in your reading?" "Have you found any books that have been difficult?" "Have they all been pretty interesting?"

In discussing some of these questions, you and the other group members will share specific things from your quiet time reading this last week.

3. Read and discuss the "How" and "Why" of using the *Bible Reading Highlights Record* (pages 37-38).

Have the students read through "How to use Your *Bible Reading Highlights Record*" going around the circle as usual. You will want to have them locate the various sections on the *Highlights Record*; for example, "translation," "year," "date," etc. They can keep one hand on a copy of the *Highlights Record* and the other hand on pages 37 and 38. The small circle by each day will be used to keep track of Scripture memory review in order to complete "Reviewed *Beginning with Christ* for 7 Consecutive Days" (see *Completion Record*, page 5).

Ask if there are any questions or comments about how to use the *Highlights Record* before going into an explanation of the reasons why (page 38). In addition to providing a transition, this will also clear up any questions before going on to new material.

Have the students continue going around the circle as they read aloud, "Why Use the *Bible Reading Highlights Record*". You might want to say something like this: "Here are some excellent reasons for using this *Highlights Record*. It is a valuable exercise and can be extremely helpful in our spiritual health and growth. Here on page 38 we will be looking at some of the benefits that have been seen in the lives of other students involved in this course, and we can expect to derive some of these same benefits as we use the *Highlights Record*. So, _____, would you please read the first one." Continue by having each of the other "Whys" read aloud by someone.

4. Discuss "The Quiet Time" (pages 38-39).

Have one person read the opening quotation and someone else read the two definitions under question 1.

Have several people each look up one verse under "two major reasons for having a quiet time" and be ready to read that verse when you request it. Each student has already looked up all the verses and written down a summary statement. You will be going over each verse and answer briefly in order to sharpen their understanding and deepen their convictions.

Have someone read "2a. For Growth and Nourishment" and the short paragraph following. Then you might say, "Let's briefly review how each of these verses indicates that the Word of God is nourishment for our spiritual lives."

Have the person who looked up 1 Peter 2:2 read the verse. Ask for a few comments as to what the verse says about growth and nourishment. Do the same for each of the verses. Then go on to "2b. For Vital Companionship with Jesus Christ" and follow the same procedure as in 2a.

5. Discuss "Quiet Time, Reading Plans, and Bible Study" (pages 39-40).

The purpose of this material is to clarify the spiritual benefits in Bible reading and Bible study and to understand their differences.

Remember that they have already read and marked this section. First ask them for some of the highlights from "1a. Bible Reading: Quiet Time". After several have shared, handle "1b. Bible Reading: Reading Plans" in the same way. Do the same with 1c. Finally, ask someone to summarize "2. Bible Study". As you can imagine, the last two will take much less time than the first two. Don't belabor these brief discussions. Keep them short and move on to the next thing.

6. Discuss how to use the *Completion Record* (page 5).

Say something like, "On the *Completion Record* you have the requirements which each of you must fulfill to graduate from this course. It will be exciting to have more and more of these categories signed off each week."

"Let me explain what each of these items means so you will see what is involved. The first five lines are probably clear. Starting tonight or in the next session, you can have some of the first five items signed. If next week you are able to say the first four passages without any mistakes (the topic, reference, verse, and the reference), then the person who hears you quote these verses can initial and date the appropriate sign off spaces."

"The field testing of this material showed that it is best not to have husbands and wives check each other. We tend to be too lenient or too strict, and there have been a few family arguments over this type of thing. So let's keep it simple and have the *Completion Record* signed by a group member outside your immediate family."

All that is necessary to get each of the five verses signed is for the person to say the topic, reference, verse, and reference sometime during a given session. If, for example, a person was unable to quote 1 Corinthians 10:13 correctly but he was able to spot where his mistake was, he could then go on to quote the other verses he wanted to quote and come back and quote 1 Corinthians 10:13. If at that time he could quote 1 Corinthians 10:13 without an error, it could be signed on the *Completion Record.*

"After having the first five spaces signed, you must wait one more week before you can complete 'Quoted all *Beginning with Christ* Verses'. This means saying all five verses without coaching or help at all, without any mistakes. The five verses do not need to be said in the order they were assigned."

"Reviewed *Beginning with Christ* for 7 consecutive days" is worked on after all five verses have been memorized. Then the student will review all five verses to himself (or to another person if he so desires) for 7 consecutive days without missing a day of reviewing all five verses. This is normally recorded on the *Highlights Record* in the circle beside the date, so another group member can simply look over the student's *Highlights Record* and see that there are seven circles consecutively marked with a check mark or an "X" to indicate that the student has completed 7 consecutive reviews of all five verses.

"Completed the *Beginning with Christ* Bible Study" can be signed off when someone looks at the material and sees that the student has filled in an answer to every question.

"Completed *Bible Reading Highlights Record* for 7 consecutive days" is very similar to "Reviewed *Beginning with Christ* for 7 consecutive days." A student must go 7 consecutive days reading and marking and writing something each day on the *Highlights Record.* This requirement can be signed off by having someone look at seven consecutive dates with entries on the *Highlights Record.* The actual entries do not need to be read.

"Bible Study." When each Bible study is completed, another group member can sign it off along with the date.

"Booklet Studied."—The *Tyranny of the Urgent* space on the *Completion Record* can be signed off when the article has been read. Also "Pages 23-24" can be signed off when this has been filled out.

The items under "Miscellaneous" can be signed off when the required work has been completed on the various pages and the student's Evangelism Prayer List has been looked at.

"Five Entries on the *Bible Reading Highlights Record*" is the place for you, as the leader, to read at least five *Highlights Record* entries for each student. This enables you to be certain that each student is recording something that is meaningful, not too introspective nor too sketchy, and not making the applications too difficult. Then make any comments you feel might help the student have a more enjoyable time in reading. In most cases you will not say any more than, "It looks as though you are having a good time in your reading; keep up the good work."

The graduation item, which is the last entry on the *Completion Record*, is self-explanatory. You can simply say to the students, "I will sign the graduation section on your *Completion Record* after you have completed all your work, and it will certify that you have graduated from this course. You should certainly be commended when you accomplish the assignments which will enable you to graduate in just a few more sessions."

7. Read the "Assignment for Session 6" (page 41).
Have one of the students read the assignment. Ask if the assignment is clear.

8. Pray.
Have someone close in prayer.

Session 6

1. Break into groups of two or three and review 1 John 5:11-12, John 16:24, 1 Corinthians 10:13, and 1 John 1:9.

Have the students break into verse review groups and quote the four passages. Encourage them to keep the verses sharp by reviewing them daily. As they learn more verses, there may be a tendency to let their review slide. Share some of your struggles and victories in Scripture memory.

2. Share highlights from your reading—particularly those which have been recorded on your *Highlights Record.*

Say something like: "Tonight we want to do our usual sharing from what we've been reading. You may either share directly from what you marked in your Bibles, or you may wish to read one or two entries from your *Highlights Records.* As we progress in the course we will get to the point where we only share from what we have actually written down on the *Highlights Record,* but for now that doesn't matter so much. Whichever way you prefer to share tonight will be fine. Take a few seconds to look over your *Highlights Record* and decide what you will share. Who would like to be first?"

In recording the "Best Thing I Marked Today," it is quickest and simplest to write down the quotation from the Scripture exactly. This eliminates the step of having to paraphrase and is an expedient method. Some of the students, however, will elect to paraphrase the main "thought" of the passage or particular verse and that is also acceptable.

In this session especially commend those who share from the *Highlights Record* by saying something like: "That's really terrific. You have recorded something that is very meaningful," or "Thank you for sharing those things."

3. Discuss the Bible study, "The Word" (pages 42-47).

Start out with a brief discussion of the "Think About" question. Simply read the question aloud yourself and ask how some of the group would answer it.

Have someone read the next paragraph. Then continue on through the lesson. As a part of your preparation, you should continue to refer back to pages 80-89 in your leader's guide.

Additional Discussion Questions for "The Word":

Question 1. Nehemiah 9:13-14—What makes the Bible unique when compared to other religious books?

Question 2. What are some ways we demonstrate our confidence in the reliability of Scripture?

Question 3a. Mark 7:6-9—What are some examples of "tradition" to which we give undue authority?

Question 3c. Luke 10:25-28—How can Scripture be used wisely when there is disagreement?

Question 4a. 2 Timothy 3:16—Give an example of how God used His Word in your life in one of these ways.

Question 7. Ezra 7:10—Define what should happen before we study the Scriptures.

4. Read and discuss the Evangelism Prayer List information (pages 47-48).
Have the students read around the circle aloud—each taking a paragraph or two. At this point they feel comfortable enough to decide how much to read. One of your goals over the weeks is to make the group less and less leader-centered.

Ask the people to make comments and observations as you go through each of the three evangelism sections. If they ask questions, direct each question to the group before you give any answer. You do not want to be known as the expert who has all the answers. You want to function as a facilitator, not as an authority figure.

5. Read the "Assignment for Session 7" (page 48).
Emphasize the importance of prayerfully and thoughtfully completing the Evangelism Prayer List. They should be aware that Satan may oppose the completion of this and that it is not uncommon for students to put this off until the last minute.

6. Pray.
Remember especially some of the thoughts from the Bible study discussion.

Session 7

1. Break into groups and review all five of the *Beginning with Christ* verses.
Have the students review together as usual and see how much they can get signed on their *Completion Records*. Say something like: "Let's break right into our verse review groups. Let's see how many things we can get signed on our *Completion Records*. Then we'll get back together."

If you have extra time, you can give them a Scripture memory mini-quiz. In rapid order throw out a mixture of verses, references, topics, and have them supply the missing ingredients. By now, they should have these pretty well down. This mini-quiz will be affirming and fun for them and for you.

2. Share highlights from your reading—particularly those which have been recorded on your *Highlights Record*.
First, give them two or three minutes of silence in which to look over their recent entries on their *Highlights Records*.

It would be good if everyone in the group could share from their *Bible Reading Highlights Record*. Don't rush the students but do keep things moving. Try not to get upset with brief silences.

Discourage their sharing just from their Bibles. You really want them to share what they actually wrote down on their *Highlights Records*. Even if they have something written on the *Highlights Record*, they may tend to ad lib their sharing rather than reading directly from it. You can set the example by going first.

In this session or the next you may agree together that you will only share from what is actually written down on the *Highlights Record*. Don't present the idea in a legalistic manner. You will find that they will respond to such a simple but important challenge.

3. Share what has impressed, helped, or challenged you during this course.

You might say something like: "We would like to take a few minutes right now to give each of you an opportunity to express some of your reactions to what you've been learning and doing in this course. We are approaching the end of the course. At this time please share with us what has most impressed, helped or challenged you during the time we have been meeting together. Feel free to share once or twice."

The purpose of this exercise is to help the students realize the benefits they have received. You will find that it is encouraging and motivational to them. Don't hurry them. Because there is no Bible study this week, there is adequate time.

4. Discuss your Evangelism Prayer List.

Have everyone get out the 3x5 card on which they have recorded their Evangelism Prayer List.

Below are some questions you could ask to stimulate discussion and assist the students to learn from one another on this assignment. The questions you choose to ask should be directed to the group, not to individuals in the group—then, individuals will answer your questions.

    a. How difficult was it for you to come up with 5-10 names of non-Christian contacts?

    b. How much did you pray and for what did you pray before you actually wrote out your list?

    c. From where do most of your names come?—Work? Neighbors? Elsewhere?

    d. How many non-Christian contacts do you have who are already close friends?

    e. What pattern do you see in the type of person you tend to gravitate to?

    f. What else did you learn or observe in your experience of making up this prayer list?

Encourage them to carry the Evangelism Prayer List as a bookmark in the Bible they are using for quiet time reading.

5. Discuss "Guide to Conversational Prayer" (pages 49-50).

As you know, they have studied this section as a part of their homework. You are going to read the section aloud for review and deepened impact before having some conversational prayer together.

You can mention to them that we want to read this section aloud in the group, make any comments or observations they may have, and then pray together conversationally.

6. Have a brief time of conversational prayer on two or three topics.

Here is an opportunity for the students to get a feel for what conversational prayer is all about. Have two or three topics in mind to pray about. Ask for their suggestions. Mention that you will participate in the conversational prayer with them and will close off the prayer time in a few minutes. Then ask someone to lead off.

7. Read the "Assignment for Session 8" (page 50).

Have someone read the assignment for Session 8.

Session 8

1. Break into groups of two or three, review all five memory verses and work on getting items initialed on your *Completion Record.*

Remind them that there are only two more sessions left to complete the course requirements. As they get together to quote the five memory passages they should also get other items initialed.

This brief review time is another opportunity for the students to review all five of the verses they have learned in this course. You will want to encourage them and challenge them to keep reviewing all of these verses every day.

When you are back together, ask how many were able to quote all five passages without a mistake. Commend those who are able to do this. You want them to establish good review habits so they will be able to retain their memory verses.

When you are back together, you will also want to ask how near some of them are to having all their course requirements signed off on their *Completion Record.* Encourage those who are a little behind to get all caught up by the next session if they possibly can.

2. Share at least one item from your *Highlights Record* with the rest of the group.

Follow the same procedure as the past several weeks. Keep the sharing moving, and praise those who do share from their *Highlights Record,* also those who share something practical and relevant to their lives.

Are you reminding them of the need to do seven consecutive verse reviews and seven consecutive *Highlights Record* entries during their quiet times?

Are you making plans to check *Highlights* within the next week or two? Remember, one of the requirements is for the leader to check *Highlights*. A way to do this would be to collect a page, take it home, and then give it back with comments and suggestions. This allows a closer, less hurried look on your part. Also, an actual written reply shows that you take this very seriously and that you are willing to write down your thoughts for their benefit.

3. Discuss the Bible study, "Prayer" (pages 51-55).

How are you doing at covering your Bible study material in the time allotted? Decide what your goals are, allocate your time carefully, and emphasize key points accordingly. Prepare your study thoroughly. The focus you put on a particular study should happen by design, not by default.

In your lesson preparation, continue to refer back to pages 80-89 in this leader's guide.

Additional Discussion Questions for "Prayer":
Question 1   What does "mercy" mean to you?
Question 1   What does "grace" mean to you?
Question 2   What do you think it means to "pour out our hearts" to God?
Question 3   What is the difference between praise and thanksgiving?
Question 4   Psalm 66:18—What is the difference between a recurring sin and a sin we cling to or cherish?

Question 4   1 John 5:14-15—What things can help us pray within God's will?
Question 6   Romans 10:1—What group would be to us today like Israel was to Paul?
Question 6   Matthew 9:37-38—How does this differ from praying for non-Christians?

4. Read the "Assignment for Session 9" (page 55).

Have a student read the assignment for Session 9.

5. Have a brief time of conversational prayer.

Ask a student to begin the period of conversational prayer. This should be a highlight of every session as the students become comfortable praying conversationally.

As you use conversational prayer, consider giving direction by suggesting some areas to pray about, such as praise, thanksgiving, forgiveness, personal problems, needs of the church, needs of others outside the group, and opportunities for sharing what they are learning.

Session 9

1. Break into groups of two or three, review all five memory verses, and work on getting items initialed on your *Completion Record*.

By now everyone should have the memory requirements completed and initialed on their *Completion Records*. They are now quoting verses they know and deepening their confidence in saying them aloud.

2. Share at least one item from your *Highlights Record* with the rest of the group.

By now you're sharing together from the Word of God should be very meaningful and personal. The sharing times will help draw the group together in an atmosphere of rich fellowship, care, and concern for one another. In most sessions you will also want to share something during this time.

3. Discuss *The Wheel Illustration* (pages 56-63).

We cannot overemphasize the relevance of *The Wheel* to everything else we have done in this course. There isn't one dimension in these materials or in the students' lives, both individually and collectively, that cannot be tied into *The Wheel*. If they continue on in *The 2:7 Series*, all of that training will also tie into *The Wheel*.

It is important for the members of your group to understand *The Wheel* and to work with it enough to be able to recall the six parts, their location, and their interrelationships.

The Wheel is an excellent yardstick for periodically taking a measurement of the balance and vitality of one's spiritual life. *The Wheel* is both a vivid illustration and a practical tool.

The Wheel Illustration is not an end in itself and is not important in itself, but the issues it represents are of utmost importance. Convey its usefulness to your group and encourage its use in order to be balanced, obedient disciples of Jesus Christ.

As you know, people in your group have already read through this material as a part of their homework. Discuss this section a page at a time, starting with page 56. You can say something like, "As you studied page _____ , What impressed you?" Or, "Who will summarize for us what page _____ says?" You don't need to belabor each page—just cover each page. "The Composite" on page 63 is perhaps the most important of these pages.

4. Discuss the Evangelism Prayer List.

In Session 6 we discussed "Why Have an Evangelism Prayer List", "Setting Up Your Evangelism Prayer List", and "Developing Contacts With Non-Christians." In Session 7, you and each of the students came to class with a prepared Evangelism Prayer List.

Now, for about 10 minutes, you will want to briefly discuss each of the following questions:
1. How consistently have you been praying for the people on your list?
2. What have you been praying for them?
3. What things have happened to deepen your friendship with some of them?
4. What other insights did you gain in making and using an Evangelism Prayer List?

By now some may have shared Christ with someone on their list. Praise God. That is wonderful, but it is beyond the goals of this course. You don't want the students to feel guilty if they have not yet shared the gospel with someone.

You want the students to do two things as a result of these three discussions on the Evangelism Prayer List.
1. You want them to identify and list their friendliest non-Christian contacts.
2. You want them to begin praying for these people.

If students go on in *The 2:7 Series,* they will be involved in further input and exercises to sharpen their evangelism effectiveness. *The 2:7 Series* will build on what they have learned and experienced with their Evangelism Prayer List in this course.

5. Discuss the Bible study, "Fellowship" (pages 64-68).

Have someone read the opening quotation. Then spend some time discussing the "Think About" question together.

Continue on through the Bible study discussion, "Fellowship."

Additional Discussion Questions for "Fellowship":

Question 2	Why is sharing so crucial to both the individual Christian and the group?
Question 4	Proverbs 27:17—How do you feel we sharpen one another as Christians?
Question 4	Ecclesiastes 4:9-10—What are some examples of two being better than one?
Question 10	Ephesians 4:11-13—What percentage of the ministry should be done by "professional" Christians? What percentage by lay people?
Question 11	James 5:16—How do you think confession to another Christian affects spiritual healing?

6. Read the "Assignment for Session 10" (page 68).

Have someone in the group read the assignment. Ask if there are any questions about the assignment.

7. Have a brief time of conversational prayer.

Suggest that this brief time of prayer be focused on the ingredients found in *The Wheel Illustration.* Ask someone to pray first and ask someone else to end the prayer time in about five minutes. This puts the responsibility on others but the guidelines are clear and definite.

Session 10

1. Break into groups of two or three, review all five memory verses, and work on getting items initialed on your *Completion Record.*

This gives them another chance to review all their memory verses. Each time they do this, the verses become sharper and the content and meaning have a greater opportunity to impact their lives.

During this time they should get the final items initialed on their *Completion Records.* This is often the session when you will initial the last two items on most of their *Completion Records.*

2. Share at least one item from your *Highlights Record.*

By now they should be feeling quite comfortable with using the *Highlights Record.* You should continue to make comments of encouragement as people share.

3. Discuss "A Personal Evaluation of *The Wheel* in My Life" (page 69).

You may handle the first two subpoints in one of two ways:

a. You can name one of the six parts of *The Wheel* and have a hand vote of those who feel strongest in that area. Go through each of the six parts and take a vote on each. Then, go on to the one in which they felt weakest. Have a vote on each of the six items for that.

b. Let them go around the circle with each sharing an answer to subpoint 1. When everyone has shared, go on to subpoint 2 and each share around the circle.

In covering subpoint 3, simply ask the group what they would like to share from that which they have written down under "Personal observations and questions." You, the group leader, should not answer the questions. Have the questions directed to the group. You, as a member of the group, can help in answering the questions. Don't be the authority figure. The discussion will be better if each person shares one observation or question at a time. They may share several times if they wish.

Subpoint 4, "Comments from others:", is simply a place to take notes as others share during the discussion.

Those who have something written under each of the first three subpoints can have someone initial "Completed the Evaluation of *The Wheel*" on their *Completion Records.*

4. Discuss "Why Memorize Scripture" (page 70).

Part 1—As the leader and a participant in the group you will have completed this assignment as the rest have.

If you have been through a leader training clinic, you will have this work previously completed. If you have the time you can always work on improving the wording so that your listed reasons communicate clearly.

Go around the circle and have each person share something written under Part 1. If the first participant says something about helping to meditate on the Scriptures, you might then ask if anyone else had a similar reason. You would then go on to the next person to see what he or she would like to share. Then see who else wrote down something similar. When it is your turn to share in the sequence of going around the circle, go ahead and share. Don't skip over yourself.

By the time you go around the second time there will be some people who have run out of things to contribute. Just allow them to pass and go on to the next person. When it gets down to one or two who still have something left to share, have one of them share whatever he or she has left. Do the same with the other person.

Do not rush during the sharing. You will want to remind the people in your group to write down on page 70 additional reasons they hear from the other people in the group. This will give everyone an expanded list of reasons for memorizing Scripture.

After the people in the group have accumulated their lists of reasons, you want to complete the segment by saying something like: "I am sure that you are convinced there are some fantastic reasons for hiding God's Word in our hearts. Scripture memory can give us some great benefits. It can help us grow spiritually. It can help equip us to minister to others."

Part 2—Have someone read question 2a.

Everyone in the group will have written in an answer or two under 2a before coming to class. Now that they have heard all the reasons given during the discussion, they may wish to write in additional reasons. Give them a chance to do this. It should take only two or three minutes. Then, go around the circle and have each person share the benefits that most motivate them. Take your turn when the sharing gets around the circle to you.

Cover 2b by asking the group what things they think could keep a person from being successful in Scripture memory. To close this off, go around the circle and have each person share one main thing that could most hinder him or her from doing well in Scripture memory.

If people in the group go on in *The 2:7 Series* they will be doing more Scripture memory. The work done on this page will help motivate them for the future and clarify to them what it will take to succeed in Scripture memory if they go on in *The 2:7 Series*.

5. Check *Completion Records*

If people have not met the course requirements, encourage them to complete them within the next two weeks. Offer to personally assist them over any hurdles they may have encountered. As the leader you will want to graduate all those who have their *Completion Records* signed off. You can do it at this point or at the end of the Session.

6. Discuss the Bible study "Witness" (pages 71-73).

Have someone read the quotation by Paul Little.

Discuss the "Think About" question. It is a fun and interesting question.

Continue on through the Bible study discussion, "Witness." This will be an excellent time to draw in some of their experiences in using the Evangelism Prayer List and relating to non-Christians.

Additional Discussion Questions for "Witness":

Question 1   Matthew 4:19—What do you think is involved in following Jesus?

Question 3a   Which of these reasons most motivates you to witness?

Question 6   Acts 20:24—What do you think developed this attitude in Paul?

Question 6   Acts 20:24—What, if anything, in this attitude do you consider extreme and what do you consider normal?

Question 6   Romans 1:15-16—What do you think are some of the reasons for our feeling embarrassed to talk about the gospel?

Question 7   Romans 10:13-15—What do you feel tends to be the weakest and the strongest link in this chain?

7. Read aloud "Keep Growing," (page 74).

This is a very important page! It commends the students for the things they have accomplished during this course. It lets them know what *The 2:7 Series* is and what it could do for them. Completing segments of *The 2:7 Series* can revolutionize their lives and ministries. We don't want to push them. We simply want them to understand *The 2:7 Series* and its tremendous value.

8. Have a brief time of conversational prayer.

Bible Reading Highlights Record

On the following pages you will find enough *Bible Reading Highlights Records* to last you through *Growing Strong in God's Family*. For an additional supply you may want to take out one of the *Bible Reading Highlights Records* before writing on it and make several copies.

My Personal Reading Record

Following the *Bible Reading Highlights Records* you will find the two-page sheet *My Personal Reading Record,* on which you will chart your progress in Bible reading. The page is perforated, so you can tear it out and keep it in your Bible. See pages 28-29 on *How to Use My Personal Reading Record.*

BIBLE READING HIGHLIGHTS RECORD

"Happy are those who keep My ways. Hear instruction and be wise, and do not refuse it. Happy is the man listening to Me, watching daily at My gates, keeping watch at My doorposts."

Proverbs 8:32-34, BERK

Translation_____ Year_____

○ **Sunday**   Date_____ All I read today_____
Best thing I marked today: *Reference:*_____
Thought: _____
_____
_____
How it impressed me:_____
_____
_____
_____
_____
_____
_____
_____

○ **Monday**   Date_____ All I read today_____
Best thing I marked today: *Reference:*_____
Thought: _____
_____
_____
How it impressed me:_____
_____
_____
_____
_____
_____
_____
_____
_____
_____

○ **Tuesday**   Date_____ All I read today_____
Best thing I marked today: *Reference:*_____
Thought: _____
_____
_____
How it impressed me:_____
_____
_____
_____
_____
_____
_____

○ **Wednesday** Date_____ All I read today_____
Best thing I marked today: *Reference:*_____
Thought: _____
_____
_____
_____
How it impressed me:_____
_____
_____
_____
_____
_____
_____
_____
_____
_____
_____

○ **Thursday**   Date_____ All I read today_____
Best thing I marked today: *Reference:*_____
Thought: _____
_____
_____
How it impressed me:_____
_____
_____
_____
_____
_____
_____
_____

○ **Friday**   Date_____ All I read today_____
Best thing I marked today: *Reference:*_____
Thought: _____
_____
_____
How it impressed me:_____
_____
_____
_____
_____
_____
_____
_____
_____

○ **Saturday**   Date_____ All I read today_____
Best thing I marked today: *Reference:*_____
Thought: _____
_____
_____
How it impressed me:_____
_____
_____
_____
_____
_____

BIBLE READING HIGHLIGHTS RECORD

"Happy are those who keep My ways. Hear instruction and be wise, and do not refuse it. Happy is the man listening to Me, watching daily at My gates, keeping watch at My doorposts."

Proverbs 8:32-34, BERK

Translation_____ Year _____

Sunday Date_____ All I read today_____
Best thing I marked today: *Reference:*_____
Thought: _____
_____
_____
How it impressed me:_____
_____
_____
_____
_____
_____
_____
_____

Monday Date_____ All I read today_____
Best thing I marked today: *Reference:*_____
Thought: _____
_____
_____
How it impressed me:_____
_____
_____
_____
_____
_____
_____
_____
_____

Tuesday Date_____ All I read today_____
Best thing I marked today: *Reference:*_____
Thought: _____
_____
_____
How it impressed me:_____
_____
_____
_____
_____
_____

Wednesday Date_____ All I read today_____
Best thing I marked today: *Reference:*_____
Thought: _____
_____
_____
_____
How it impressed me:_____
_____
_____
_____
_____
_____
_____
_____
_____

Thursday Date_____ All I read today_____
Best thing I marked today: *Reference:*_____
Thought: _____
_____
_____
How it impressed me:_____
_____
_____
_____
_____
_____
_____
_____

Friday Date_____ All I read today_____
Best thing I marked today: *Reference:*_____
Thought: _____
_____
_____
How it impressed me:_____
_____
_____
_____
_____
_____
_____
_____
_____

Saturday Date_____ All I read today_____
Best thing I marked today: *Reference:*_____
Thought: _____
_____
_____
How it impressed me:_____
_____
_____
_____
_____
_____

BIBLE READING HIGHLIGHTS RECORD

"Happy are those who keep My ways. Hear instruction and be wise, and do not refuse it. Happy is the man listening to Me, watching daily at My gates, keeping watch at My doorposts."

Proverbs 8:32-34, BERK

*Translation*_____ *Year*_____

Sunday　　Date_____ All I read today_____
Best thing I marked today: *Reference:*_____
*Thought:*_____
_____
_____
How it impressed me:_____
_____
_____
_____
_____
_____
_____
_____
_____
_____

Monday　　Date_____ All I read today_____
Best thing I marked today: *Reference:*_____
*Thought:*_____
_____
How it impressed me:_____
_____
_____
_____
_____
_____
_____
_____
_____

Tuesday　　Date_____ All I read today_____
Best thing I marked today: *Reference:*_____
*Thought:*_____
_____
_____
How it impressed me:_____
_____
_____
_____
_____
_____

Wednesday Date_____ All I read today_____
Best thing I marked today: *Reference:*_____
*Thought:*_____
_____
_____
_____
How it impressed me:_____
_____
_____
_____
_____
_____
_____
_____
_____
_____

Thursday　　Date_____ All I read today_____
Best thing I marked today: *Reference:*_____
*Thought:*_____
_____
How it impressed me:_____
_____
_____
_____
_____
_____
_____
_____
_____

Friday　　Date_____ All I read today_____
Best thing I marked today: *Reference:*_____
*Thought:*_____
_____
How it impressed me:_____
_____
_____
_____
_____
_____
_____
_____

Saturday　　Date_____ All I read today_____
Best thing I marked today: *Reference:*_____
*Thought:*_____
_____
_____
How it impressed me:_____
_____
_____
_____
_____
_____

BIBLE READING HIGHLIGHTS RECORD

"Happy are those who keep My ways. Hear instruction and be wise, and do not refuse it. Happy is the man listening to Me, watching daily at My gates, keeping watch at My doorposts."

Proverbs 8:32-34, BERK

Translation_____ Year_____

○ **Sunday** Date_____ All I read today_____
Best thing I marked today: *Reference:*_____
*Thought:*_____
_____
_____
_____

How it impressed me:_____
_____
_____
_____
_____
_____
_____
_____
_____

○ **Monday** Date_____ All I read today_____
Best thing I marked today: *Reference:*_____
*Thought:*_____
_____
_____
_____

How it impressed me:_____
_____
_____
_____
_____
_____
_____
_____
_____

○ **Tuesday** Date_____ All I read today_____
Best thing I marked today: *Reference:*_____
*Thought:*_____
_____
_____
_____

How it impressed me:_____
_____
_____
_____
_____
_____

○ **Wednesday** Date_____ All I read today_____
Best thing I marked today: *Reference:*_____
*Thought:*_____
_____
_____
_____
_____
_____

How it impressed me:_____
_____
_____
_____
_____
_____
_____
_____
_____
_____
_____
_____

○ **Thursday** Date_____ All I read today_____
Best thing I marked today: *Reference:*_____
*Thought:*_____
_____
_____
_____

How it impressed me:_____
_____
_____
_____
_____
_____
_____
_____
_____

○ **Friday** Date_____ All I read today_____
Best thing I marked today: *Reference:*_____
*Thought:*_____
_____
_____
_____

How it impressed me:_____
_____
_____
_____
_____
_____
_____
_____
_____

○ **Saturday** Date_____ All I read today_____
Best thing I marked today: *Reference:*_____
*Thought:*_____
_____
_____
_____

How it impressed me:_____
_____
_____
_____
_____

BIBLE READING HIGHLIGHTS RECORD

"Happy are those who keep My ways. Hear instruction and be wise, and do not refuse it. Happy is the man listening to Me, watching daily at My gates, keeping watch at My doorposts."

Proverbs 8:32-34, BERK

Translation _____ *Year* _____

○ **Sunday** Date _____ All I read today _____
Best thing I marked today: *Reference:* _____
Thought: _____
_____
_____
How it impressed me: _____
_____
_____
_____
_____
_____
_____
_____

○ **Monday** Date _____ All I read today _____
Best thing I marked today: *Reference:* _____
Thought: _____
_____
_____
How it impressed me: _____
_____
_____
_____
_____
_____
_____
_____

○ **Tuesday** Date _____ All I read today _____
Best thing I marked today: *Reference:* _____
Thought: _____
_____
_____
How it impressed me: _____
_____
_____
_____
_____
_____
_____

○ **Wednesday** Date _____ All I read today _____
Best thing I marked today: *Reference:* _____
Thought: _____
_____
_____
_____
How it impressed me: _____
_____
_____
_____
_____
_____
_____
_____
_____
_____

○ **Thursday** Date _____ All I read today _____
Best thing I marked today: *Reference:* _____
Thought: _____
_____
_____
How it impressed me: _____
_____
_____
_____
_____
_____
_____
_____

○ **Friday** Date _____ All I read today _____
Best thing I marked today: *Reference:* _____
Thought: _____
_____
_____
How it impressed me: _____
_____
_____
_____
_____
_____
_____
_____

○ **Saturday** Date _____ All I read today _____
Best thing I marked today: *Reference:* _____
Thought: _____
_____
_____
How it impressed me: _____
_____
_____
_____
_____
_____

BIBLE READING HIGHLIGHTS RECORD

"Happy are those who keep My ways. Hear instruction and be wise, and do not refuse it. Happy is the man listening to Me, watching daily at My gates, keeping watch at My doorposts."

Proverbs 8:32-34, BERK

*Translation*_____ *Year*_____

○ **Sunday** Date_____ All I read today_____
Best thing I marked today: *Reference:*_____
*Thought:*_____
_____
_____
_____
How it impressed me:_____
_____
_____
_____
_____
_____
_____
_____
_____

○ **Monday** Date_____ All I read today_____
Best thing I marked today: *Reference:*_____
*Thought:*_____
_____
_____
_____
How it impressed me:_____
_____
_____
_____
_____
_____
_____
_____
_____

○ **Tuesday** Date_____ All I read today_____
Best thing I marked today: *Reference:*_____
*Thought:*_____
_____
_____
_____
How it impressed me:_____
_____
_____
_____
_____
_____
_____

○ **Wednesday** Date_____ All I read today_____
Best thing I marked today: *Reference:*_____
*Thought:*_____
_____
_____
_____
_____
How it impressed me:_____
_____
_____
_____
_____
_____
_____
_____
_____
_____
_____

○ **Thursday** Date_____ All I read today_____
Best thing I marked today: *Reference:*_____
*Thought:*_____
_____
_____
_____
How it impressed me:_____
_____
_____
_____
_____
_____
_____
_____
_____

○ **Friday** Date_____ All I read today_____
Best thing I marked today: *Reference:*_____
*Thought:*_____
_____
_____
_____
How it impressed me:_____
_____
_____
_____
_____
_____
_____

○ **Saturday** Date_____ All I read today_____
Best thing I marked today: *Reference:*_____
*Thought:*_____
_____
_____
_____
How it impressed me:_____
_____
_____
_____
_____
_____
_____

BIBLE READING HIGHLIGHTS RECORD

"Happy are those who keep My ways. Hear instruction and be wise, and do not refuse it. Happy is the man listening to Me, watching daily at My gates, keeping watch at My doorposts."

Proverbs 8:32-34, BERK

Translation _____ *Year* _____

○ **Sunday** Date _____ All I read today _____
Best thing I marked today: *Reference:* _____
Thought: _____
_____
_____
How it impressed me: _____
_____
_____
_____
_____
_____
_____

○ **Monday** Date _____ All I read today _____
Best thing I marked today: *Reference:* _____
Thought: _____
_____
_____
How it impressed me: _____
_____
_____
_____
_____
_____
_____

○ **Tuesday** Date _____ All I read today _____
Best thing I marked today: *Reference:* _____
Thought: _____
_____
_____
How it impressed me: _____
_____
_____
_____
_____

○ **Wednesday** Date _____ All I read today _____
Best thing I marked today: *Reference:* _____
Thought: _____
_____
_____
How it impressed me: _____
_____
_____
_____
_____
_____
_____
_____
_____

○ **Thursday** Date _____ All I read today _____
Best thing I marked today: *Reference:* _____
Thought: _____
_____
_____
How it impressed me: _____
_____
_____
_____
_____
_____
_____

○ **Friday** Date _____ All I read today _____
Best thing I marked today: *Reference:* _____
Thought: _____
_____
_____
How it impressed me: _____
_____
_____
_____
_____
_____
_____

○ **Saturday** Date _____ All I read today _____
Best thing I marked today: *Reference:* _____
Thought: _____
_____
_____
How it impressed me: _____
_____
_____
_____
_____

BIBLE READING HIGHLIGHTS RECORD

"Happy are those who keep My ways. Hear instruction and be wise, and do not refuse it. Happy is the man listening to Me, watching daily at My gates, keeping watch at My doorposts."

Proverbs 8:32-34, BERK

*Translation*_____ *Year* _____

○ **Sunday** Date_____ All I read today_____
Best thing I marked today: *Reference:*_____
*Thought:*_____
_____
_____
How it impressed me:_____
_____
_____
_____
_____
_____
_____
_____

○ **Monday** Date_____ All I read today_____
Best thing I marked today: *Reference:*_____
*Thought:*_____
_____
_____
How it impressed me:_____
_____
_____
_____
_____
_____
_____
_____

○ **Tuesday** Date_____ All I read today_____
Best thing I marked today: *Reference:*_____
*Thought:*_____
_____
_____
How it impressed me:_____
_____
_____
_____
_____
_____

○ **Wednesday** Date_____ All I read today_____
Best thing I marked today: *Reference:*_____
*Thought:*_____
_____
_____
_____
How it impressed me:_____
_____
_____
_____
_____
_____
_____
_____
_____
_____

○ **Thursday** Date_____ All I read today_____
Best thing I marked today: *Reference:*_____
*Thought:*_____
_____
_____
How it impressed me:_____
_____
_____
_____
_____
_____
_____
_____

○ **Friday** Date_____ All I read today_____
Best thing I marked today: *Reference:*_____
*Thought:*_____
_____
_____
How it impressed me:_____
_____
_____
_____
_____
_____
_____
_____

○ **Saturday** Date_____ All I read today_____
Best thing I marked today: *Reference:*_____
*Thought:*_____
_____
_____
How it impressed me:_____
_____
_____
_____
_____
_____

BIBLE READING HIGHLIGHTS RECORD

"Happy are those who keep My ways. Hear instruction and be wise, and do not refuse it. Happy is the man listening to Me, watching daily at My gates, keeping watch at My doorposts."

Proverbs 8:32-34, BERK

Translation_____ Year _____

○ **Sunday** Date_____ All I read today_____
Best thing I marked today: *Reference:*_____
*Thought:*_____
_____
_____

How it impressed me:_____
_____
_____
_____
_____
_____
_____

○ **Monday** Date_____ All I read today_____
Best thing I marked today: *Reference:*_____
*Thought:*_____
_____
_____

How it impressed me:_____
_____
_____
_____
_____
_____
_____
_____

○ **Tuesday** Date_____ All I read today_____
Best thing I marked today: *Reference:*_____
*Thought:*_____
_____
_____

How it impressed me:_____
_____
_____
_____
_____
_____

○ **Wednesday** Date_____ All I read today_____
Best thing I marked today: *Reference:*_____
*Thought:*_____
_____
_____

How it impressed me:_____
_____
_____
_____
_____
_____
_____
_____
_____

○ **Thursday** Date_____ All I read today_____
Best thing I marked today: *Reference:*_____
*Thought:*_____
_____
_____

How it impressed me:_____
_____
_____
_____
_____
_____
_____

○ **Friday** Date_____ All I read today_____
Best thing I marked today: *Reference:*_____
*Thought:*_____
_____
_____

How it impressed me:_____
_____
_____
_____
_____
_____

○ **Saturday** Date_____ All I read today_____
Best thing I marked today: *Reference:*_____
*Thought:*_____
_____
_____

How it impressed me:_____
_____
_____
_____
_____
_____

BIBLE READING HIGHLIGHTS RECORD

"Happy are those who keep My ways. Hear instruction and be wise, and do not refuse it. Happy is the man listening to Me, watching daily at My gates, keeping watch at My doorposts."

Proverbs 8:32-34, BERK

*Translation*_____ *Year* _____

○ **Sunday** Date_____ All I read today_____
Best thing I marked today: *Reference:*_____
Thought: _____
_____
_____
How it impressed me:_____
_____
_____
_____
_____
_____
_____
_____
_____

○ **Monday** Date_____ All I read today_____
Best thing I marked today: *Reference:*_____
Thought: _____
_____
_____
How it impressed me:_____
_____
_____
_____
_____
_____
_____
_____
_____

○ **Tuesday** Date_____ All I read today_____
Best thing I marked today: *Reference:*_____
Thought: _____
_____
_____
How it impressed me:_____
_____
_____
_____
_____
_____
_____

○ **Wednesday** Date_____ All I read today_____
Best thing I marked today: *Reference:*_____
Thought: _____
_____
_____
How it impressed me:_____
_____
_____
_____
_____
_____
_____
_____
_____
_____

○ **Thursday** Date_____ All I read today_____
Best thing I marked today: *Reference:*_____
Thought: _____
_____
_____
How it impressed me:_____
_____
_____
_____
_____
_____
_____
_____
_____

○ **Friday** Date_____ All I read today_____
Best thing I marked today: *Reference:*_____
Thought: _____
_____
_____
How it impressed me:_____
_____
_____
_____
_____
_____
_____
_____

○ **Saturday** Date_____ All I read today_____
Best thing I marked today: *Reference:*_____
Thought: _____
_____
_____
How it impressed me:_____
_____
_____
_____
_____

BIBLE READING HIGHLIGHTS RECORD

"Happy are those who keep My ways. Hear instruction and be wise, and do not refuse it. Happy is the man listening to Me, watching daily at My gates, keeping watch at My doorposts."

Proverbs 8:32-34, BERK

*Translation*_____ *Year* _____

○ **Sunday** Date_____ All I read today_____
Best thing I marked today: *Reference:*_____
Thought: _____
_____
_____

How it impressed me:_____
_____
_____
_____
_____
_____
_____
_____

○ **Monday** Date_____ All I read today_____
Best thing I marked today: *Reference:*_____
Thought: _____
_____
_____
_____

How it impressed me:_____
_____
_____
_____
_____
_____
_____
_____

○ **Tuesday** Date_____ All I read today_____
Best thing I marked today: *Reference:*_____
Thought: _____
_____
_____
_____

How it impressed me:_____
_____
_____
_____
_____
_____

○ **Wednesday** Date_____ All I read today_____
Best thing I marked today: *Reference:*_____
Thought: _____
_____
_____

How it impressed me:_____
_____
_____
_____
_____
_____
_____
_____

○ **Thursday** Date_____ All I read today_____
Best thing I marked today: *Reference:*_____
Thought: _____
_____
_____
_____

How it impressed me:_____
_____
_____
_____
_____
_____

○ **Friday** Date_____ All I read today_____
Best thing I marked today: *Reference:*_____
Thought: _____
_____
_____

How it impressed me:_____
_____
_____
_____
_____
_____

○ **Saturday** Date_____ All I read today_____
Best thing I marked today: *Reference:*_____
Thought: _____
_____
_____

How it impressed me:_____
_____
_____
_____
_____

BIBLE READING HIGHLIGHTS RECORD

"Happy are those who keep My ways. Hear instruction and be wise, and do not refuse it. Happy is the man listening to Me, watching daily at My gates, keeping watch at My doorposts."

Proverbs 8:32-34, BERK

*Translation*_____ *Year*_____

○ **Sunday** Date_____ All I read today_____
Best thing I marked today: *Reference:*_____
*Thought:*_____
_____
_____
How it impressed me:_____
_____
_____
_____
_____
_____

○ **Monday** Date_____ All I read today_____
Best thing I marked today: *Reference:*_____
*Thought:*_____
_____
_____
How it impressed me:_____
_____
_____
_____
_____
_____
_____

○ **Tuesday** Date_____ All I read today_____
Best thing I marked today: *Reference:*_____
*Thought:*_____
_____
_____
How it impressed me:_____
_____
_____
_____
_____

○ **Wednesday** Date_____ All I read today_____
Best thing I marked today: *Reference:*_____
*Thought:*_____
_____
_____
_____
How it impressed me:_____
_____
_____
_____
_____
_____
_____
_____
_____

○ **Thursday** Date_____ All I read today_____
Best thing I marked today: *Reference:*_____
*Thought:*_____
_____
_____
How it impressed me:_____
_____
_____
_____
_____
_____

○ **Friday** Date_____ All I read today_____
Best thing I marked today: *Reference:*_____
*Thought:*_____
_____
_____
How it impressed me:_____
_____
_____
_____
_____
_____

○ **Saturday** Date_____ All I read today_____
Best thing I marked today: *Reference:*_____
*Thought:*_____
_____
_____
How it impressed me:_____
_____
_____
_____
_____

BIBLE READING HIGHLIGHTS RECORD

"Happy are those who keep My ways. Hear instruction and be wise, and do not refuse it. Happy is the man listening to Me, watching daily at My gates, keeping watch at My doorposts."

Proverbs 8:32-34, BERK

*Translation*_____ *Year* _____

○ **Sunday**   Date_____ All I read today_____
Best thing I marked today: *Reference:*_____
Thought: _____
_____
_____
How it impressed me:_____
_____
_____
_____
_____
_____
_____
_____
_____

○ **Monday**   Date_____ All I read today_____
Best thing I marked today: *Reference:*_____
Thought: _____
_____
_____
How it impressed me:_____
_____
_____
_____
_____
_____
_____
_____
_____

○ **Tuesday**   Date_____ All I read today_____
Best thing I marked today: *Reference:*_____
Thought: _____
_____
_____
How it impressed me:_____
_____
_____
_____
_____
_____

○ **Wednesday** Date_____ All I read today_____
Best thing I marked today: *Reference:*_____
Thought: _____
_____
_____
_____
How it impressed me:_____
_____
_____
_____
_____
_____
_____
_____
_____
_____
_____

○ **Thursday**   Date_____ All I read today_____
Best thing I marked today: *Reference:*_____
Thought: _____
_____
_____
How it impressed me:_____
_____
_____
_____
_____
_____
_____
_____
_____

○ **Friday**   Date_____ All I read today_____
Best thing I marked today: *Reference:*_____
Thought: _____
_____
_____
How it impressed me:_____
_____
_____
_____
_____
_____
_____
_____
_____

○ **Saturday**   Date_____ All I read today_____
Best thing I marked today: *Reference:*_____
Thought: _____
_____
_____
How it impressed me:_____
_____
_____
_____
_____
_____

BIBLE READING HIGHLIGHTS RECORD

"Happy are those who keep My ways. Hear instruction and be wise, and do not refuse it. Happy is the man listening to Me, watching daily at My gates, keeping watch at My doorposts."

Proverbs 8:32-34, BERK

*Translation*_____ **Year**_____

○ **Sunday** Date_____ All I read today_____
Best thing I marked today: *Reference:*_____
*Thought:*_____
_____
_____
How it impressed me:_____
_____
_____
_____
_____
_____
_____
_____

○ **Monday** Date_____ All I read today_____
Best thing I marked today: *Reference:*_____
*Thought:*_____
_____
_____
How it impressed me:_____
_____
_____
_____
_____
_____
_____
_____
_____

○ **Tuesday** Date_____ All I read today_____
Best thing I marked today: *Reference:*_____
*Thought:*_____
_____
_____
How it impressed me:_____
_____
_____
_____
_____

○ **Wednesday** Date_____ All I read today_____
Best thing I marked today: *Reference:*_____
*Thought:*_____
_____
_____
_____
How it impressed me:_____
_____
_____
_____
_____
_____
_____
_____
_____
_____

○ **Thursday** Date_____ All I read today_____
Best thing I marked today: *Reference:*_____
*Thought:*_____
_____
How it impressed me:_____
_____
_____
_____
_____
_____
_____
_____

○ **Friday** Date_____ All I read today_____
Best thing I marked today: *Reference:*_____
*Thought:*_____
_____
_____
How it impressed me:_____
_____
_____
_____
_____
_____
_____

○ **Saturday** Date_____ All I read today_____
Best thing I marked today: *Reference:*_____
*Thought:*_____
_____
_____
How it impressed me:_____
_____
_____
_____
_____

BIBLE READING HIGHLIGHTS RECORD

"Happy are those who keep My ways. Hear instruction and be wise, and do not refuse it. Happy is the man listening to Me, watching daily at My gates, keeping watch at My doorposts."

Proverbs 8:32-34, BERK

Translation_____ Year _____

Sunday   Date_____ All I read today_____
Best thing I marked today: *Reference:*_____
Thought: _____
_____
_____
How it impressed me:_____
_____
_____
_____
_____
_____
_____
_____

Monday   Date_____ All I read today_____
Best thing I marked today: *Reference:*_____
Thought: _____
_____
_____
How it impressed me:_____
_____
_____
_____
_____
_____
_____
_____

Tuesday   Date_____ All I read today_____
Best thing I marked today: *Reference:*_____
Thought: _____
_____
_____
How it impressed me:_____
_____
_____
_____
_____

Wednesday Date_____ All I read today_____
Best thing I marked today: *Reference:*_____
Thought: _____
_____
_____
_____
How it impressed me:_____
_____
_____
_____
_____
_____
_____
_____
_____
_____

Thursday   Date_____ All I read today_____
Best thing I marked today: *Reference:*_____
Thought: _____
_____
_____
How it impressed me:_____
_____
_____
_____
_____
_____
_____
_____

Friday   Date_____ All I read today_____
Best thing I marked today: *Reference:*_____
Thought: _____
_____
_____
How it impressed me:_____
_____
_____
_____
_____
_____
_____
_____

Saturday   Date_____ All I read today_____
Best thing I marked today: *Reference:*_____
Thought: _____
_____
_____
How it impressed me:_____
_____
_____
_____
_____

BIBLE READING HIGHLIGHTS RECORD

"Happy are those who keep My ways. Hear instruction and be wise, and do not refuse it. Happy is the man listening to Me, watching daily at My gates, keeping watch at My doorposts."

Proverbs 8:32-34, BERK

*Translation*_____ *Year* _____

○ **Sunday**   Date_____ All I read today_____
Best thing I marked today: *Reference:*_____
Thought: _____
_____
_____
How it impressed me:_____
_____
_____
_____
_____
_____
_____
_____
_____

○ **Monday**   Date_____ All I read today_____
Best thing I marked today: *Reference:*_____
Thought: _____
_____
_____
How it impressed me:_____
_____
_____
_____
_____
_____
_____

○ **Tuesday**   Date_____ All I read today_____
Best thing I marked today: *Reference:*_____
Thought: _____
_____
_____
How it impressed me:_____
_____
_____
_____
_____
_____

○ **Wednesday** Date_____ All I read today_____
Best thing I marked today: *Reference:*_____
Thought: _____
_____
_____
_____
How it impressed me:_____
_____
_____
_____
_____
_____
_____
_____
_____
_____

○ **Thursday**   Date_____ All I read today_____
Best thing I marked today: *Reference:*_____
Thought: _____
_____
_____
How it impressed me:_____
_____
_____
_____
_____
_____
_____
_____

○ **Friday**   Date_____ All I read today_____
Best thing I marked today: *Reference:*_____
Thought: _____
_____
_____
How it impressed me:_____
_____
_____
_____
_____
_____
_____

○ **Saturday**   Date_____ All I read today_____
Best thing I marked today: *Reference:*_____
Thought: _____
_____
_____
How it impressed me:_____
_____
_____
_____
_____
_____

BIBLE READING HIGHLIGHTS RECORD

"Happy are those who keep My ways. Hear instruction and be wise, and do not refuse it. Happy is the man listening to Me, watching daily at My gates, keeping watch at My doorposts."

Proverbs 8:32-34, BERK

Translation_____ Year _____

Sunday Date_____ All I read today_____
Best thing I marked today: *Reference:*_____
Thought: _____
_____
_____
How it impressed me:_____
_____
_____
_____
_____
_____

Monday Date_____ All I read today_____
Best thing I marked today: *Reference:*_____
Thought: _____
_____
_____
How it impressed me:_____
_____
_____
_____
_____
_____

Tuesday Date_____ All I read today_____
Best thing I marked today: *Reference:*_____
Thought: _____
_____
_____
How it impressed me:_____
_____
_____
_____
_____
_____

Wednesday Date_____ All I read today_____
Best thing I marked today: *Reference:*_____
Thought: _____
_____
_____
How it impressed me:_____
_____
_____
_____
_____
_____
_____
_____
_____

Thursday Date_____ All I read today_____
Best thing I marked today: *Reference:*_____
Thought: _____
_____
_____
How it impressed me:_____
_____
_____
_____
_____
_____

Friday Date_____ All I read today_____
Best thing I marked today: *Reference:*_____
Thought: _____
_____
_____
How it impressed me:_____
_____
_____
_____
_____
_____

Saturday Date_____ All I read today_____
Best thing I marked today: *Reference:*_____
Thought: _____
_____
_____
How it impressed me:_____
_____
_____
_____
_____

BIBLE READING HIGHLIGHTS RECORD

"Happy are those who keep My ways. Hear instruction and be wise, and do not refuse it. Happy is the man listening to Me, watching daily at My gates, keeping watch at My doorposts."

Proverbs 8:32-34, BERK

Translation_____ Year_____

○ **Sunday** Date_____ All I read today_____
Best thing I marked today: *Reference:*_____
*Thought:*_____
_____
_____
How it impressed me:_____
_____
_____
_____
_____
_____

○ **Monday** Date_____ All I read today_____
Best thing I marked today: *Reference:*_____
*Thought:*_____
_____
_____
How it impressed me:_____
_____
_____
_____
_____
_____
_____
_____

○ **Tuesday** Date_____ All I read today_____
Best thing I marked today: *Reference:*_____
*Thought:*_____
_____
_____
How it impressed me:_____
_____
_____
_____
_____
_____

○ **Wednesday** Date_____ All I read today_____
Best thing I marked today: *Reference:*_____
*Thought:*_____
_____
_____
_____
_____
How it impressed me:_____
_____
_____
_____
_____
_____
_____
_____
_____

○ **Thursday** Date_____ All I read today_____
Best thing I marked today: *Reference:*_____
*Thought:*_____
_____
_____
How it impressed me:_____
_____
_____
_____
_____
_____

○ **Friday** Date_____ All I read today_____
Best thing I marked today: *Reference:*_____
*Thought:*_____
_____
_____
How it impressed me:_____
_____
_____
_____
_____
_____

○ **Saturday** Date_____ All I read today_____
Best thing I marked today: *Reference:*_____
*Thought:*_____
_____
_____
How it impressed me:_____
_____
_____
_____

BIBLE READING HIGHLIGHTS RECORD

"Happy are those who keep My ways. Hear instruction and be wise, and do not refuse it. Happy is the man listening to Me, watching daily at My gates, keeping watch at My doorposts."

Proverbs 8:32-34, BERK

Translation_____ Year_____

○ **Sunday**   Date_____ All I read today_____
Best thing I marked today: *Reference:*_____
Thought: _____
_____
_____
How it impressed me:_____
_____
_____
_____
_____
_____
_____

○ **Monday**   Date_____ All I read today_____
Best thing I marked today: *Reference:*_____
Thought: _____
_____
_____
How it impressed me:_____
_____
_____
_____
_____
_____
_____

○ **Tuesday**   Date_____ All I read today_____
Best thing I marked today: *Reference:*_____
Thought: _____
_____
_____
How it impressed me:_____
_____
_____
_____
_____

○ **Wednesday** Date_____ All I read today_____
Best thing I marked today: *Reference:*_____
Thought: _____
_____
_____
_____
How it impressed me:_____
_____
_____
_____
_____
_____
_____
_____
_____

○ **Thursday**   Date_____ All I read today_____
Best thing I marked today: *Reference:*_____
Thought: _____
_____
How it impressed me:_____
_____
_____
_____
_____
_____
_____

○ **Friday**   Date_____ All I read today_____
Best thing I marked today: *Reference:*_____
Thought: _____
_____
How it impressed me:_____
_____
_____
_____
_____
_____

○ **Saturday**   Date_____ All I read today_____
Best thing I marked today: *Reference:*_____
Thought: _____
_____
How it impressed me:_____
_____
_____
_____
_____

BIBLE READING HIGHLIGHTS RECORD

"Happy are those who keep My ways. Hear instruction and be wise, and do not refuse it. Happy is the man listening to Me, watching daily at My gates, keeping watch at My doorposts."

Proverbs 8:32-34, BERK

Translation_____ Year_____

○ **Sunday** Date_____ All I read today_____
Best thing I marked today: *Reference:*_____
Thought: _____
_____
_____
How it impressed me:_____
_____
_____
_____
_____
_____
_____
_____
_____

○ **Monday** Date_____ All I read today_____
Best thing I marked today: *Reference:*_____
Thought: _____
_____
_____
How it impressed me:_____
_____
_____
_____
_____
_____
_____
_____
_____

○ **Tuesday** Date_____ All I read today_____
Best thing I marked today: *Reference:*_____
Thought: _____
_____
_____
How it impressed me:_____
_____
_____
_____
_____
_____

○ **Wednesday** Date_____ All I read today_____
Best thing I marked today: *Reference:*_____
Thought: _____
_____
_____
_____
How it impressed me:_____
_____
_____
_____
_____
_____
_____
_____
_____
_____
_____

○ **Thursday** Date_____ All I read today_____
Best thing I marked today: *Reference:*_____
Thought: _____
_____
_____
How it impressed me:_____
_____
_____
_____
_____
_____
_____
_____
_____

○ **Friday** Date_____ All I read today_____
Best thing I marked today: *Reference:*_____
Thought: _____
_____
_____
How it impressed me:_____
_____
_____
_____
_____
_____
_____
_____
_____

○ **Saturday** Date_____ All I read today_____
Best thing I marked today: *Reference:*_____
Thought: _____
_____
_____
How it impressed me:_____
_____
_____
_____
_____
_____

MY PERSONAL READING RECORD

Genesis	1	2	3	4	5	6	7	8	9	10	11	12	13	14	15	16	17	18	19	20
	21	22	23	24	25	26	27	28	29	30	31	32	33	34	35	36	37	38	39	40
	41	42	43	44	45	46	47	48	49	50										
Exodus	1	2	3	4	5	6	7	8	9	10	11	12	13	14	15	16	17	18	19	20
	21	22	23	24	25	26	27	28	29	30	31	32	33	34	35	36	37	38	39	40
Leviticus	1	2	3	4	5	6	7	8	9	10	11	12	13	14	15	16	17	18	19	20
	21	22	23	24	25	26	27													
Numbers	1	2	3	4	5	6	7	8	9	10	11	12	13	14	15	16	17	18	19	20
	21	22	23	24	25	26	27	28	29	30	31	32	33	34	35	36					
Deuteronomy	1	2	3	4	5	6	7	8	9	10	11	12	13	14	15	16	17	18	19	20
	21	22	23	24	25	26	27	28	29	30	31	32	33	34							
Joshua	1	2	3	4	5	6	7	8	9	10	11	12	13	14	15	16	17	18	19	20
	21	22	23	24																
Judges	1	2	3	4	5	6	7	8	9	10	11	12	13	14	15	16	17	18	19	20
	21																			
Ruth	1	2	3	4																
1 Samuel	1	2	3	4	5	6	7	8	9	10	11	12	13	14	15	16	17	18	19	20
	21	22	23	24	25	26	27	28	29	30	31									
2 Samuel	1	2	3	4	5	6	7	8	9	10	11	12	13	14	15	16	17	18	19	20
	21	22	23	24																
1 Kings	1	2	3	4	5	6	7	8	9	10	11	12	13	14	15	16	17	18	19	20
	21	22																		
2 Kings	1	2	3	4	5	6	7	8	9	10	11	12	13	14	15	16	17	18	19	20
	21	22	23	24	25															
1 Chronicles	1	2	3	4	5	6	7	8	9	10	11	12	13	14	15	16	17	18	19	20
	21	22	23	24	25	26	27	28	29											
2 Chronicles	1	2	3	4	5	6	7	8	9	10	11	12	13	14	15	16	17	18	19	20
	21	22	23	24	25	26	27	28	29	30	31	32	33	34	35	36				
Ezra	1	2	3	4	5	6	7	8	9	10										
Nehemiah	1	2	3	4	5	6	7	8	9	10	11	12	13							
Esther	1	2	3	4	5	6	7	8	9	10										
Job	1	2	3	4	5	6	7	8	9	10	11	12	13	14	15	16	17	18	19	20
	21	22	23	24	25	26	27	28	29	30	31	32	33	34	35	36	37	38	39	40
	41	42																		
Psalms	1	2	3	4	5	6	7	8	9	10	11	12	13	14	15	16	17	18	19	20
	21	22	23	24	25	26	27	28	29	30	31	32	33	34	35	36	37	38	39	40
	41	42	43	44	45	46	47	48	49	50	51	52	53	54	55	56	57	58	59	60
	61	62	63	64	65	66	67	68	69	70	71	72	73	74	75	76	77	78	79	80
	81	82	83	84	85	86	87	88	89	90	91	92	93	94	95	96	97	98	99	100
	101	102	103	104	105	106	107	108	109	110	111	112	113	114	115	116	117	118	119	120
	121	122	123	124	125	126	127	128	129	130	131	132	133	134	135	136	137	138	139	140
	141	142	143	144	145	146	147	148	149	150										
Proverbs	1	2	3	4	5	6	7	8	9	10	11	12	13	14	15	16	17	18	19	20
	21	22	23	24	25	26	27	28	29	30	31									
Ecclesiastes	1	2	3	4	5	6	7	8	9	10	11	12								
Song of Songs	1	2	3	4	5	6	7	8												
Isaiah	1	2	3	4	5	6	7	8	9	10	11	12	13	14	15	16	17	18	19	20
	21	22	23	24	25	26	27	28	29	30	31	32	33	34	35	36	37	38	39	40
	41	42	43	44	45	46	47	48	49	50	51	52	53	54	55	56	57	58	59	60
	61	62	63	64	65	66														
Jeremiah	1	2	3	4	5	6	7	8	9	10	11	12	13	14	15	16	17	18	19	20
	21	22	23	24	25	26	27	28	29	30	31	32	33	34	35	36	37	38	39	40
	41	42	43	44	45	46	47	48	49	50	51	52								
Lamentations	1	2	3	4	5															
Ezekiel	1	2	3	4	5	6	7	8	9	10	11	12	13	14	15	16	17	18	19	20
	21	22	23	24	25	26	27	28	29	30	31	32	33	34	35	36	37	38	39	40
	41	42	43	44	45	46	47	48												

Daniel	1	2	3	4	5	6	7	8	9	10	11	12		
Hosea	1	2	3	4	5	6	7	8	9	10	11	12	13	14
Joel	1	2	3											
Amos	1	2	3	4	5	6	7	8	9					
Obadiah	1													
Jonah	1	2	3	4										
Micah	1	2	3	4	5	6	7							
Nahum	1	2	3											
Habakkuk	1	2	3											
Zephaniah	1	2	3											
Haggai	1	2												
Zechariah	1	2	3	4	5	6	7	8	9	10	11	12	13	14
Malachi	1	2	3	4										

New Testament

Matthew	1	2	3	4	5	6	7	8	9	10	11	12	13	14	15	16	17	18	19	20
	21	22	23	24	25	26	27	28												
Mark	1	2	3	4	5	6	7	8	9	10	11	12	13	14	15	16				
Luke	1	2	3	4	5	6	7	8	9	10	11	12	13	14	15	16	17	18	19	20
	21	22	23	24																
John	1	2	3	4	5	6	7	8	9	10	11	12	13	14	15	16	17	18	19	20
	21																			
Acts	1	2	3	4	5	6	7	8	9	10	11	12	13	14	15	16	17	18	19	20
	21	22	23	24	25	26	27	28												
Romans	1	2	3	4	5	6	7	8	9	10	11	12	13	14	15	16				
1 Corinthians	1	2	3	4	5	6	7	8	9	10	11	12	13	14	15	16				
2 Corinthians	1	2	3	4	5	6	7	8	9	10	11	12	13							
Galatians	1	2	3	4	5	6														
Ephesians	1	2	3	4	5	6														
Philippians	1	2	3	4																
Colossians	1	2	3	4																
1 Thessalonians	1	2	3	4	5															
2 Thessalonians	1	2	3																	
1 Timothy	1	2	3	4	5	6														
2 Timothy	1	2	3	4																
Titus	1	2	3																	
Philemon	1																			
Hebrews	1	2	3	4	5	6	7	8	9	10	11	12	13							
James	1	2	3	4	5															
1 Peter	1	2	3	4	5															
2 Peter	1	2	3																	
1 John	1	2	3	4	5															
2 John	1																			
3 John	1																			
Jude	1																			
Revelation	1	2	3	4	5	6	7	8	9	10	11	12	13	14	15	16	17	18	19	20
	21	22																		

"And now, brethren, I commend you to God, and to the Word of His grace, which is able to build you up, and to give you an inheritance among all them which are sanctified."—Acts 20:32

Congratulations!

You've successfully completed *Growing Strong in God's Family!* To recognize your diligence and concern for discipleship, The Navigators would like to send you a special new book—at a special price.

Trusting God, from Jerry Bridges (author of *The Pursuit of Holiness*), uncovers three essential truths about God—truths we must believe if we are to trust Him in adversity. They are:

- God is completely sovereign.
- God is infinite in wisdom.
- God is perfect in love.

"In order to trust God," writes Bridges, "we must always view our adverse circumstances through the eyes of faith, not of sense. When we seek Him in the midst of personal pain and discover Him to be trustworthy, we'll find ourselves in a deeper, more intimate relationship with Him as a result."

We are not at the mercy of circumstances. Although God's ways of working in our lives are frequently beyond explanation, we must learn to trust Him. Even when we don't understand.

This hard-hitting book is one you'll want to refer to frequently for a long time to come. And, because of the commitment you've demonstrated to pursuing a deeper, more intimate relationship with God, The Navigators would like to send you *Trusting God* for only $6.95— a $2 savings off its regular cover price.

Simply check the appropriate box on the card inserted into this book, and mail it to us with your payment. Thanks—and congratulations!

CHURCH DISCIPLESHIP MINISTRIES

This is the division of The Navigators that seeks to make discipleship a reality in the local church. CDM staff and associates throughout the United States help local churches maximize their effectiveness in discipleship and outreach.

NAVPRESS

Helping Christians grow by engaging them in Bible studies and heart-level reading is the mission of NavPress. Our distinctive areas of expertise include evangelism, follow-up, discipleship, Bible study & memory aids, women's materials, and tools for churches and small groups.

DISCIPLESHIP JOURNAL

This full-color, bimonthly magazine goes beyond reliable Bible teaching to help you *apply* what you read. Bible studies and discussion questions following most of the articles encourage you to dig deeper and take specific action based on what you've learned.

Each issue contains a theme section that gives you a closer look at one aspect of living for Christ. These sections are ideal for in-depth personal studies and serve as excellent resource material for small group studies.

Discipleship Journal also offers you a special section devoted to helping your small group be a more significant means of growing spiritually. Once offered as a subscription newsletter, "The Small Group Letter" is now available only inside the *Journal*.

THE NAVIGATORS' DAILY WALK

This monthly Bible reading guide is the perfect supplement to your Bible Reading Highlights Record. You'll be led through the entire Bible in one exciting year—with helpful overviews, maps, and charts that make the journey a vivid experience.

THE NAVIGATORS' CLOSER WALK

Just like *Daily Walk*, this supplemental Bible reading guide is a powerful resource. But only the New Testament becomes your text for the year—affording you a more leisurely pace, yet with the same lively approach. An ideal choice for busy adults.

SMALL-GROUP MATERIALS FROM NAVPRESS

BIBLE STUDY SERIES

CRISISPOINTS FOR WOMEN
DESIGN FOR DISCIPLESHIP
GOD IN YOU
GOD'S DESIGN FOR THE FAMILY

LIFECHANGE
LIFESTYLE SMALL GROUP SERIES
QUESTIONS WOMEN ASK
STUDIES IN CHRISTIAN LIVING

TOPICAL BIBLE STUDIES

Adam, Out of Eden
Becoming a Woman of
   Excellence
The Blessing Study Guide
Caring Without Wearing
Celebrating Life
The Creator, My Confidant
Crystal Clear
Eve, Out of Eden

Growing in Christ
Growing Strong in God's Family
Homemaking
A Mother's Legacy
Surviving Life in the Fast Lane
To Run and Not Grow Tired
To Walk and Not Grow Weary
When the Squeeze Is On

BIBLE STUDIES WITH COMPANION BOOKS

Hiding from Love
Inside Out
The Practice of Godliness
The Pursuit of Holiness
Secret Passions of the Christian
   Woman

Transforming Grace
Trusting God
Your Work Matters to God

RESOURCES

Curriculum Resource Guide
How to Lead Small Groups
Jesus Cares for Women
The Small Group Leaders
   Training Course

Topical Memory System (KJV/NIV
   and NASB/NKJV)

VIDEO PACKAGES

Abortion
Edge TV
Hope Has Its Reasons
Inside Out

Living Proof
Parenting Adolescents
Your Home, A Lighthouse